About the Author

Manitoba author Don Aiken was born in Winnipeg but spent much of his youth in Scotland. As a teenager he landed a job on a cattle-boat and, subsequently, saw much of the world from the deck of a freighter. On his return to Winnipeg, Aiken attended Normal School and then taught in a one-room schoolhouse near Duck Mountain. During the Second World War he joined the RCAF and trained navigators at Rivers, Manitoba, prior to going overseas himself, also as a navigator.

Aiken spent much of his adult life employed in the newspaper industry. Most of his years in journalism were spent with the *Winnipeg Tribune*, but from 1961 to 1966 he was editor of the *Dryden Observer*. With the "Trib" Don was, at various times, copyeditor, editorial page editor, and book editor. A love of history and literature, combined with his work as a book editor, allowed Aiken to create a home library that would be the envy of many communities.

A widower with three children, eight grandchildren, and four great-grandchildren, Don is also an accomplished poet.

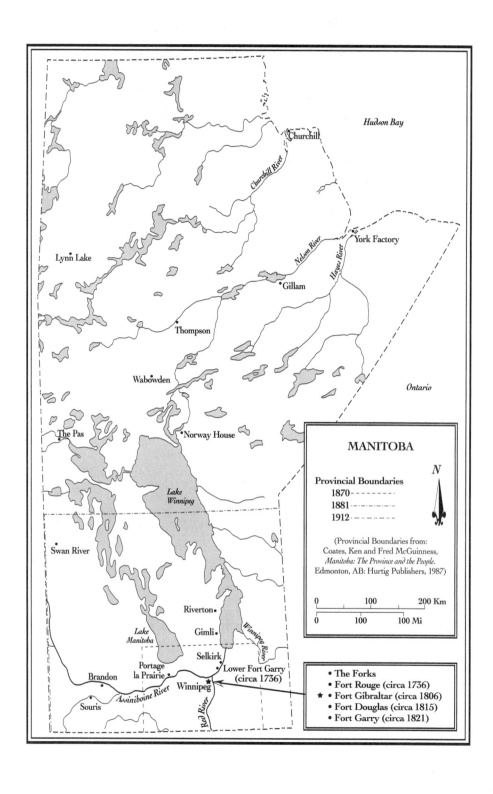

Hudson Bay

Churchill

York Factory

Ontario

Lynn Lake

Gillam

Thompson

Wabowden

The Pas

Norway House

Lake Winnipeg

Swan River

Riverton

Lake Manitoba

Gimli

Selkirk

Portage la Prairie

Brandon

Souris

Winnipeg

Lower Fort Garry (circa 1736)

Churchill River

Nelson River

Hayes River

Winnipeg River

Red River

Assiniboine River

MANITOBA

N

Provincial Boundaries
1870 ----------
1881 ----------
1912 ----------

(Provincial Boundaries from:
Coates, Ken and Fred McGuinness,
Manitoba: The Province and the People.
Edmonton, AB: Hurtig Publishers, 1987)

0   100   200 Km
0   100   100 Mi

- **The Forks**
- **Fort Rouge (circa 1736)**
★ • **Fort Gibraltar (circa 1806)**
- **Fort Douglas (circa 1815)**
- **Fort Garry (circa 1821)**

It Happened in Manitoba
Stories of the Red River Province

Don Aiken

with Chris Thain

FIFTH
HOUSE

Cover and interior design by Kathy Aldous-Schleindl
Cover illustration: view of Winnipeg from St. Boniface Ferry Landing, 1882, Glenbow Archives (NA-1041-1); colourized with permission
Back cover photograph of the Elks Jazz Band courtesy Archives of Manitoba (N1888)
Edited by Alex Frazer-Harrison
Copyedited by Meaghan Craven
Proofread by Joan Tetrault
Scans by St. Solo Computer Graphics

The publisher gratefully acknowledges the support of The Canada Council for the Arts and the Department of Canadian Heritage.

 Canada Council   Conseil des Arts
for the Arts   du Canada

We acknowledge the financial support of the Government of Canada through the Book Publishing Industry Development Program for our publishing activities.

Printed in Canada by Friesens

04 05 06 07 08 / 5 4 3 2 1

First published in the United States in 2004 by Fitzhenry & Whiteside
121 Harvard Avenue, Suite 2
Allston, MA 02134

National Library of Canada Cataloguing in Publication Data
Aiken, Don, 1914-
    It happened in Manitoba : stories of the Red River province / by Don Aiken.
Includes index.
Collection of articles from author's column, "Heritage Highlights",
    originally published in the Winnipeg real estate news.
ISBN 1-894856-39-2
    1. Manitoba—History. I. Title.
FC3361.A34 2004   971.27   C2004-900530-8

Fifth House Ltd.
A Fitzhenry & Whiteside Company
1511, 1800-4 St. SW
Calgary, Alberta T2S 2S5

1-800-387-9776
www.fitzhenry.ca

Contents

Acknowledgements

I wish to thank the *Winnipeg Real Estate News* for the opportunity to write the body of articles from which those in this book were chosen. Thanks also to all those who encouraged and assisted me over the years with ideas and research and to all who have responded so positively to the published articles.

I wish to thank all of the staff at Fifth House Ltd. Thanks to Charlene Dobmeier, publisher, who read the original articles and approved publication. A special thanks goes to Alex Frazer-Harrison for his excellent work as editor, a job made more difficult as he had to work initially from photocopies of tear sheets. Thanks also to Senior Editors Liesbeth Leatherbarrow and Lesley Reynolds.

Most particularly I wish to thank Chris Thain. Without him this book could not have been published. Over the years many have suggested a collection of the articles but it was he who brought them to the attention of Fifth House Ltd. after that firm had published his book, *Cold as a Bay Street Banker's Heart*. He provided the computer-age communication unavailable to an aging newspaperman with his portable typewriter. And, most particularly, he undertook the search for pictures and much of the required proofreading when, unfortunately, I was unable to do so.

Introduction

The *Winnipeg Real Estate News* (WREN) has a long-standing tradition of frequently including in its weekly publication of available real estate a brief article related to Manitoba history. These articles appear under the caption, "Heritage Highlights." In the 1970s, while still employed as an editor by the *Winnipeg Tribune*, and after I had written some historical articles for that paper, I was asked by the *Winnipeg Real Estate News* to contribute articles for use as Heritage Highlights.

As this was an opportunity to pursue my love for history, particularly local history, I jumped at the chance. In the early years full-time employment limited the time available for the task and my contributions were infrequent. However, on retirement it was with great pleasure that I was able to devote the necessary time to the research and writing that resulted in my contributions becoming a regular occurrence in the WREN until the late 1990s.

In all, over 160 of my Heritage Highlights were published. With each publication came a measure of public response indicative of a general interest in history, particularly local history. The telephone conversations, meetings, and exchange of letters with all those who contacted me as a result of the articles were, and remain, a very real reward for my efforts.

Particularly appreciated were two groups of responses. One group came from those who started by saying they had disliked history as a subject in school but who then went on to say how much they had enjoyed a particular article. In this regard the WREN is to be commended for taking history to a wider audience than would have been achieved by other means. The second group of responses came from individuals related to, or whose relatives had been friends of, someone central to a story. Their comments added interesting personal family remembrances and reactions to historic events.

Please remember that the articles I wrote for the WREN were written over many years and in an order different from that of the chapters of this book. This means each chapter can be read individually but also, when the chapters are read consecutively, there will be the occasional repetition of information that is not meant to impugn the reader's short-term memory.

That said, I hope you will enjoy these glimpses of Manitoba history.

A Manitoba Winter

Sir Thomas Button led an expedition in 1612 that included the first recorded wintering by Europeans on Hudson Bay. Loss of life that winter was so great that only one of his two ships could return to England.

When the snow drives in dense clouds before wild northwest winds; when the sun shines brilliantly but the temperature is −40 (by whichever scale you want to use) and the wind chill is far worse; when tree branches crack and every living thing with any morsel of sense is holed up somewhere warm; in short, when we are enduring our severest winter weather, we should think about how well off we are in comparison with the first Europeans to winter in what is now Manitoba.

Europeans ventured into the uncharted northern waters in search of a Northwest Passage, the sought after route that would give easy access to the fabled riches of Cathay, Cipango, and the Spice Islands.

Henry Hudson and the crew of *Discovery* were the first Europeans known to have entered the bay that now bears his name. When they first saw that body of water in 1610 they thought that they had entered the Pacific. They soon discovered otherwise, and in November of that year the *Discovery* became trapped in ice in what is now James Bay. The crew wintered ashore with minimal loss of life until the ship came free in mid-June 1611.

Not much is known of that wintering as Hudson did not make it back to England. As soon as his ship was free from the ice, Hudson wanted to continue the search for the Northwest Passage, but many of the crew wanted to go home. When Hudson refused to end the search, a mutiny occurred and he, his son, and several members of the crew were put over the side in a small boat. They were never seen again.

Discovery made it home with the mutineers, all but one of whom later stood trial for the mutiny. One sailor, Robert Bylot, was pardoned for his role in bringing the ship home safely, and both he and *Discovery*, together with a second ship, *Resolution*, headed back in 1912 in an expedition lead by Thomas Button. Backed by the Company of Merchant Adventurers and bankrolled by royalty, nobility, and some of the wealthiest men in England, Button returned to Hudson Bay and resumed the search abandoned by Hudson's crew.

After exploring the western shore of Hudson Bay, Button realized he had reached a dead end. He anchored his ships in a place he called Hope Check't and decided to stop briefly to rest the crews and do some repairs before sailing home. However, he had misjudged winter's arrival. Before he knew it, Arctic gales started to blow, the snow came, and ice formed in the river and bay. The ships were hauled into a small creek on the north side of the river, and Button had his men build dikes around them to prevent the ice from crushing the hulls. Men from Europe faced the unknown of a northern winter for the second time and for the first time in what is now Manitoba.

With the long cold months and poor food came scurvy, the scourge of seamen of that time. A disease resulting from a lack of Vitamin C, scurvy causes debilitating physical conditions including severe deterioration of the gums and the loss of teeth. For centuries the disease had sapped sailors' strength and will to keep going when away from fresh food supplies for a long period of time. So many of Button's men died of scurvy, the cold, and general malnutrition that, in the spring of 1613, he was forced to leave *Resolution* behind and return to England in *Discovery*. Among those who died was *Resolution*'s sailing master, Francis Nelson, for whom the newly discovered Nelson River was named.

From 1614 to 1619 other explorers, including Robert Bylot who had served with both Hudson and Button, searched unsuccessfully for a shortcut to the East. But many still believed that it must exist. In 1619 Jens Monk, regarded as one of the best officers in the Danish-Norwegian navy, was ordered to find the passage and sailed with two ships and sixty-four men in May of that year. Faulty navigational equipment and other problems meant Monk was unable to locate Hudson Strait and the entrance to Hudson Bay until the fall. Finally, at the mouth of the Churchill River, winter caught Monk as it had Button.

In the weeks before Christmas, Monk kept his men active as they built protective barriers around the ships. But all too soon the cold weather and inadequate diet took their toll. Scurvy appeared and levied an even greater toll on Monk's company than it had on Button's crew. It was a miserable winter during which most of his sailors died. By June, when the ice sealing the anchorage vanished, only Monk and two of his men had survived out of the original complement of sixty-four.

Monk selected one of the two ships and the three survivors set out to the northeast to begin what must surely be one of history's epic sea voyages. The intrepid trio overcame all the perils of Hudson Bay,

Hudson Strait, and the Atlantic Ocean before finally reaching safe haven in Norway.

Such were the first recorded winterings by Europeans in what is now Manitoba. Over the next century, to the south across the forests between Lake Superior and the Red River, other explorers, traders, and settlers also faced their times of peril and grim adversity. But they always knew there was a relatively safe way to get back to the settlements of the St. Lawrence River.

Those of us who today feel hard done by when the car has to be plugged in, or when snow drifts into the driveway and makes it a little difficult to get to work, to shops, or to the theatre, don't know how lucky we are. We have it soft.

The Bachelor Party

Pierre Radisson, one of those who challenged the HBC in the
Hudson Bay area, greets Indians with whom he will trade.

The next time you are in the Museum of Man and Nature in Winnipeg, go to the *Nonsuch* Gallery and take a good look at the ship that sits high and dry in a make-believe dock. The ship is a full-sized replica of the original *Nonsuch*, which, under the command of Captain Zachariah Gillam, brought the first Hudson's Bay Company (HBC) traders to James Bay in 1668 and back to London in 1669. Subsequent *Nonsuch* voyages resulted in the establishment of HBC trading posts on Hudson Bay, the first at York Factory at the mouth of the Hayes River in what is now northern Manitoba.

Pierre Radisson, one of the renegade Frenchmen who helped found the HBC, and Gillam played further roles in the story of the fur trade, with some aspects of their exploits being reminiscent of comic opera or farce.

Radisson went to England in the early 1660s with the idea of trading directly between Europe and Hudson Bay because of a disagreement he had with the governor of New France. But, soon after the HBC was formed, Radisson changed sides again, managed to get back into the good books of French officialdom in Montreal and Quebec, and set off with a couple of ships to raid the HBC's monopoly territory.

In 1682 Radisson built a rough fort about 16 kilometres (10 mi.) inland on the Hayes River and proceeded to trade for furs. It wasn't long before he discovered that his was not the only party challenging the HBC monopoly. Another group of interlopers was on the Nelson River, consisting of fourteen young men from Boston who were busy gathering furs under the leadership of Ben Gillam—Zachariah's son—and a first mate who bore the appropriate name of John Lawless. Their ship was called the *Bachelor's Delight* and their base was named Bachelor's Island; it would seem that they were quite pleased with their unwed state.

Radisson was a wily and resourceful entrepreneur whose Native skills and ingenuity had been honed by a couple of years as a prisoner-adoptee of the Iroquois. From the fragmentary accounts of his experiences, it is possible to piece together the amazing and amusing sequence of events that followed Radisson's discovery of the bachelors.

Radisson decided to approach Ben Gillam's fort, introduce himself, and try to play the bachelors along as far as he could. He went to Gillam's base and persuaded Gillam and his colleagues that they all shared a common cause in their freebooting raid on HBC territory. Although he had only a small party, Radisson made Gillam believe that he had established a strong base in the territory and that he had many armed men. Radisson went on to offer them full protection from the "warlike" Indians. The Natives of the region, far from rushing about in anger and bloodlust, were only interested in trading their furs for beads, knives, axes, and cloth—trade goods of which the white men had apparently inexhaustible supplies.

Radisson had just finished his successful hoodwinking of the Gillam party when, just as in the movies, another complication arose in the form of a third ship, a vessel belonging to the HBC bearing the newly appointed governor of Rupert's Land, William Bridgar, and captained by none other than young Ben's father, Zachariah.

Radisson decided on a gigantic bluff. He sent a message to Bridgar, forbidding him to land. He had, he announced, claimed the whole territory for the King of France, brushing aside British King Charles II's charter to the HBC. Radisson claimed he was prepared—with his four hundred armed men in a strategically placed fort—to contest the HBC's claims.

Bridgar's expedition was for trade and was unequipped for military purposes, so Bridgar stayed on his ship. But Radisson knew that if Bridgar made contact with the local Indians the presence of the two poaching parties would be revealed. He had to move fast. He gambled that Zachariah Gillam's loyalty to his son would be stronger than his ties to the HBC. He thus arranged a meeting between father and son during which the astonished father did exactly what Radisson had hoped and decided against denouncing Ben to the governor.

Radisson's next step was to deal with the bachelor party. He slipped two members of his crew into Ben Gillam's fort, then surrounded the fort with his small band and, when his infiltrators opened the fort gate, seized the place. However, one of Ben's men got away and managed to reach Bridgar's ship, where he told all. Bridgar was annoyed and, with more courage than good sense, had himself rowed ashore where he marched into Radisson's fort to reassert the English claim. Bridgar immediately became a hostage, and Radisson lost no time in persuading Zachariah Gillam that things might go ill both for his son and for the governor unless he and his ship surrendered.

Soon Radisson had four ships, a governor, two captains, and two large loads of fur as his reward for a winter of trading and temerity. He looked over the ships; decided the *Bachelor's Delight* was the best of the small flotilla; loaded it with Governor Bridgar, all the Boston poachers, and all the furs; and sailed for Quebec City. He also allowed Zachariah and his small crew to proceed to the HBC post at Rupert House on James Bay.

As poet Robert Burns would note a century later, the best-laid plans go awry. Expecting a triumphant return to New France, Radisson reported to the governor upon his arrival in Quebec. To his shock and chagrin he was not only reprimanded but also had to stand by, powerless, while his furs were seized. Unknown to the adventurer, peace had been achieved between England and France during his absence and he was penalized for having attacked the ships of a friendly nation.

Radisson departed hastily from New France, no doubt thinking it prudent to get away before someone thought up new charges to bring against him. He made his way back to England where, as an expert in the gathering of furs from the Natives of Hudson Bay, he was reappointed to a position with the HBC. He persuaded his nephew to join him when he negotiated the surrender of his fort (Fort Bourbon) on the Hayes River and then became director of trade at Fort Nelson for two years.

He was uneasy on this side of the Atlantic, however, because the government of New France had put a price on his head. He returned to England where he wrote the story of his adventures and, according to the records, blew a generous pension given to him by King Charles. He died in relative poverty and obscurity in 1710.

Watercraft Across the West

The York boat, shown here on the Saskatchewan River at The Pas, was developed at York Factory to provide transportation that was safer than canoes on the rough waters of Lake Winnipeg and northern rivers.

Before the railway was laid, water was the chief medium of transportation in Canada. The first Europeans to reach this country's eastern shores started exploring its mysterious waterways using stoutly built—but cumbersome—boats, which they had brought on their ocean-going ships. They soon adopted—no doubt with mixed pleasure and trepidation—the watercraft of the Natives, the canoe.

Built of cedar frames with a skin of birch bark, sewn and caulked, canoes were light, manoeuvrable, and easy to carry where rapids or waterfalls made navigation dangerous. And if a canoe was damaged, the forest generally provided sufficient materials for repair.

Canoe-making skills were handed down from one generation of Natives to the next. Youngsters learned how to select the wood for the frames; how to soak it and bend it to the right shape; how to strip the bark from birch trees; how to find the pine roots with which the sheets of bark were sewn together; how to fit the outer skin onto the frame; and how to seal the joints with spruce or pine resin.

The voyageurs who powered the great fur brigades from the west to Hudson Bay or to Montreal adapted the canoe to their special needs. The brigades that took trade goods west from Montreal used the big craft known as *canot du maître*, which was up to 12 metres (40 ft.) long and able to take a cargo of 2,300 kilograms (5,000 lb.). It required a crew of as many as twelve, with a bowman, or *avant*, selecting the route (especially in rapid water), and a steersman, or *gouvernail*, operating the big steering paddle in the rear.

When the big canoes reached Fort William at the head of Lake Superior loads were transferred to smaller craft known as *canot du nord*. These were about half the size of the *canot du maître*, with crews of five or six and loads of up to 1,360 kilograms (3,000 lb.). The smaller canoes were necessary in the western regions because of the smaller rivers and lakes and the need for more frequent portages around rapids and falls.

The big canoes were the trademark of the North West Company fur traders and brigades from Montreal. From their trading posts on Hudson

Bay, the Hudson's Bay Company had also used canoes on their limited voyages inland but, as early as 1749, had started to develop another type of water transport vehicle that better suited the big inland lakes of what is now Manitoba and the comparatively smooth Red and Saskatchewan Rivers.

This was the York boat, first constructed at York Factory on Hudson Bay's southern coast. Skilled boat builders from the Orkney Islands of Scotland were brought over to design and build these vessels, which, with their shallow draft, great length, and long raked prow and stern, were hauntingly reminiscent of Viking long ships.

The York boat was less liable to ice damage and was safer in rough weather than the canoe. Early York boats measured about 9.1 metres (30 ft.) along the keel and had a total length of 12.6 metres (41 ft.). With approximately the same size of crew as the *canot du maître* and a carrying capacity of almost twice the lighter craft, York boats gave their users a distinct advantage in freighting costs. They were propelled by long sweeps but were also equipped with masts and sails.

The first York boats were used on the Albany River and later became the most commonly used HBC craft on the lakes and rivers of the west. Since they were made of sawed lumber, York boats could be constructed anywhere there were trees suitable for sawing into planks and heavy frame timbers. As early as 1795 they were being constructed at Fort Edmonton. York boats, built in three standard sizes for various uses, were still in use at the start of the twentieth century.

The smallest was called the 60-piece boat because it could carry 60 of the standard-sized bundles of furs or trade goods, each weighing about 45 kilograms (100 lb.). Its capacity was, therefore, 2,700 kilograms (6,000 lb.). The 100-piece boat had a capacity of 4,535 kilograms (10,000 lb.), and the largest boat in the series could carry 5,440 kilograms (12,000 lb.).

Steam power and the internal combustion engine spelled the end of the York-boat era; by the 1920s they were no longer in use. A few enthusiasts on the Red River and Lake Winnipeg later revived the York boat for recreational purposes, and races using this type of old vessel were held annually at Gimli for many years.

Both the canoe and the York boat have a solid place in Canadian culture; however it is the canoe that is best remembered. The songs of the voyageurs such as "*Youpe, Youpe su la rivière*" and poems like Pauline Johnson's "Song My Paddle Sings" and J. G. Whittier's "Red River Voyageur" contain early references to these vessels.

The paintings of Frances Ann Hopkins and others established the images of the canoe and York boat in the public consciousness, and popular history books, such as those by Pierre Berton and Peter C. Newman, placed the importance of water-borne trade on the permanent record.

Not only did trade goods, hardy boatmen, and fur traders travel the northern waters in canoes and York boats. In 1856, when Dr. William Cowan, HBC medical officer at Fort Garry, was transferred to Moose Factory on James Bay, his wife and two small children went with him on the more than 1,900-kilometre (1,200-mi.) journey that lasted four weeks and was done in a 9-metre (30-ft.) *canot du nord*.

"Our luggage and supplies had to be as light as possible," Mrs. Cowan recalled later. "Our heavy trunks were sent to York Factory to be taken in the Company ship to England and brought back across the Atlantic to us by the ship coming to Moose Factory."

The Cowans' return trip, six years later, took two months because the weather was bad and the boatmen had to tow the canoe for miles against the current of the Albany River, a process called "tracking." The trunks again made the return voyage to Fort Garry by way of England.

York boats came in handy in 1852 when the Red River flooded and they were used to move large numbers of people to higher ground and to herd livestock to safety.

Another recollection of those early days of water transport comes from Mrs. Bernard Ross, who was born in 1826 at Norway House. She recalled travelling from Norway House back to Red River with a number of other people in an HBC sloop and two York boats. "The day we were to have arrived at Berens River, there was a terrible storm on Lake Winnipeg, which was long remembered. The sloop was lost and our boats were wrecked," she said. "I was sitting beside Miss Greenleaf who had just arrived from England on her way to join her missionary brother. The boat turned upside down. One of the men saved me as I was going down." Sadly, Miss Greenleaf drowned. The survivors managed to reach a sandbar and were finally able to proceed after the boatmen salvaged one boat in which they made the rest of the trip up the lake and Red River to Fort Garry.

It is not so long ago that travel between two locations, now only hours apart, involved long, arduous, and frequently dangerous journeys in crude boats on unpredictable waterways.

The Falcon Was an Adventurer

John Tanner, raised by Indians who called him
"the Falcon," led the attack on Fort Douglas.

The small group of men, muffled in blanket coats, fur hats, and leggings, cautiously made its way through the snow toward the silent palisades of the fort. Their guns were slung on their backs and, as they plowed through the drifts in the dark of the night, they dragged trees whose branches had been cut off a foot or so from the trunks.

At the base of the wooden palisade, they halted and stood silent, looking and listening for a challenge or for any sign of watchfulness from within. Only a curl of smoke, quickly blown to tatters by the searching wind, rose from a chimney within the fort to show it was occupied.

The men raised the tree trunks until the tops rested against the upright timbers; then, after another wary pause and some whispered words, they began to climb, using the stubs of branches as one would the rungs of a ladder. There was another pause at the top and another fast scan of the interior of the fort before they dropped quickly to the ground and fanned out to the few log buildings within the walls. The men opened doors roughly, routed out the sleeping occupants at gunpoint, and herded them into the space at the centre of the fort.

While the prisoners protested, complained, and argued loudly in a mixture of English, French, Native tongues, and Scottish dialects, one of the victors brought a Native woman and a small boy from one of the buildings with a cry of triumph. The prisoners were placed under guard in one of the houses, and the captors of the fort proceeded to search the place and to refresh themselves with whatever food and drink came to hand.

Fort Douglas, the Selkirk settlement's stronghold near the forks of the Red and Assiniboine Rivers, was thus recaptured from the North West Company's men who had seized it the previous summer. Accounts of this bloodless coup vary slightly in detail, but there is general agreement that the basic tactics involved were the work of one man, John Tanner, who led the small invading party.

Tanner, who was called the "Falcon" by the Indians with whom he lived, was a member of a well-to-do family in Kentucky and Virginia. His parents were Joseph and Mary Tanner, who came from England in 1660 and settled first in Virginia but, like many settlers in the early eighteenth century, moved west to Kentucky where John was born in 1781.

At the age of eight, Tanner was kidnapped in one of the frequent raids carried out by Indian bands in an effort to try and halt the European invasion of their territory. He was taken to Saginong on the west shore of Lake Huron and traded for two kegs of whisky to Net-no-kwa, an Ottawa tribeswoman. Her husband, Big Hunter, trained young John in woods craft, hunting, reverence for nature, and the Native way of life.

In the 1790s a considerable number of Natives, mostly Saulteaux, moved from the Sault Ste. Marie area and made their way to the Red River where they settled in the Netley Creek district. Big Hunter and Net-no-kwa were in the group, as was John Tanner. Also in the party was a man who was later to figure prominently in the history of the Red River Valley, Chief Peguis. These immigrants formed an alliance with the nearby Assiniboine against the Sioux, who were encroaching from the south. Later, when the first groups of Selkirk settlers appeared in the valley from 1812 to 1815, young men of the Netley band, including Tanner, hunted buffalo to provide meat for the settlers.

Tanner trapped, traded, and explored along the Assiniboine River and in northwest Ontario and was originally considered an ally and supporter of the North West Company. However, he disagreed with the Nor'Westers' trading practices and went to work for the Hudson's Bay Company. This change of allegiance had a great effect on his life and caused a family rift.

In about 1800 Tanner had married a young Cree woman, Miskwabunokwa (The Red Sky of Morning), and they had three children: a son, Picheito (Little Pheasant), and two daughters. Some of Miskwabunokwa's family opposed Tanner's move to the HBC, and when Tanner suddenly decided to seek out his original family in the United States Miskwabunokwa left him. She returned to him on several occasions for short periods but always left again.

In about 1816, one of Miskwabunokwa's returns coincided with an attack on the settlement by the Nor'Westers' Métis members, led by Cuthbert Grant. This attack resulted in the Battle of Seven Oaks during which Governor Robert Semple and nineteen of his men were killed and Fort Douglas was captured. Miskwabunokwa and Picheito were held prisoner in the fort.

Tanner was in the Lake Superior area during the attack and the battle. When the ex-soldiers of the de Meurons regiment (hired by Lord Selkirk to recover the colony's lands) came to Tanner seeking someone to guide them, he took the job. Tanner brought them by lake, river, and portage to the Red River Valley where they won back the settlement's lands and forts in 1817.

Earlier, in about 1811, during one of Miskwabunokwa's absences, Tanner went to Sault Ste. Marie and took a second wife, Terezia, by whom he had six children. It is said that Miskwabunokwa was more than a little annoyed by her husband's bigamy and offered a warrior one of her daughters if he would find and kill Tanner. The warrior is said to have shot the Falcon and left him wounded on an island in the Rainy River district. Tanner's own version of this story was that an unnamed Native man abducted one of Tanner's daughters and, when confronted, shot the father and fled.

A party of fur traders, including Cuthbert Grant, found Tanner. The records show that Grant was able to remove the bullet from Tanner's body and help him recover. Since this well-documented event occurred in 1823, more than twelve years after Tanner and his first wife originally separated, Tanner's version of the story is probably the correct one.

Tanner eventually returned to the United States. He found that his original family was living in Georgia and was quite wealthy. Tanner's father, deceased by then, had believed his son dead and had made no provision for him in his will. The family welcomed their long-lost relative, however, and for a short time the Falcon tried to live the life of a well-to-do gentleman. But he was unhappy there and eventually returned north.

He lived in Detroit for a year or so where he married for a third time to a young white woman who bore him a daughter. No information is available about what happened to his earlier marriage with Terezia. This new marriage also did not last; his wife left him, alienated by Tanner's increasingly moody behaviour.

Tanner returned to the Sault Ste. Marie area where he took yet another wife in 1843, a Saulteaux named Geseikokwa. They had no children. Tanner lived in the Sault district for the rest of his life.

As a result of his experiences and long life with the Natives, Tanner became an ardent believer in Native spiritual values and, in later years, fiercely resisted efforts to convert him to Christianity. For this and other reasons, he was not on good terms with his white neighbours at the

Sault. When one of them, James Schoolcraft, was shot and his house burned to the ground sometime around 1846, Tanner disappeared. He was immediately blamed for the shooting and an unsuccessful search for him was undertaken.

It was not until a year after his disappearance that Tanner's body and rifle were found in a slough. Years later, a United States Army officer who had been stationed in the Sault garrison confessed on his deathbed to the Schoolcraft murder. Many believed that he also killed Tanner.

The Necessary Indian

*Chief Peguis, the renowned Indian leader of the
early 1800s, as portrayed by William Tkach.*

All Winnipeggers know the name Peguis because of the major east-west roadway in the north end of the city, Chief Peguis Trail. Manitobans outside Winnipeg relate the great chief's name to the Indian reserve bearing his name located 140 kilometres (90 mi.) north of Winnipeg on the Fisher River. The man behind the name was one of the most colourful and enigmatic of all of Manitoba's pioneers.

Peguis, a member of the Saulteaux, came to what is now Manitoba as a young man with a band of his people from Sault Ste. Marie in the 1790s. The group found unoccupied land at the point where Netley Creek enters the Red River and settled there. They called the smaller stream Death River because the original Plains Cree inhabitants had been wiped out by smallpox.

As chief of his small band, Peguis was involved in many of the dramatic events that ultimately led to the establishment of the Selkirk settlement and the formation of the province of Manitoba. Perhaps because he and his people were themselves newcomers to the land, Peguis helped and sometimes gave protection to the Selkirk settlers. He was especially helpful to the settlers after the Battle of Seven Oaks in 1816, when the Métis and the North West Company were intent on wiping them out. When the settlement's sponsor, Lord Selkirk, arrived in 1817 to re-establish his agricultural colony, Peguis and three other chiefs signed a treaty—the first of its kind in Western Canada—giving settlers the right to occupy and farm the land along the Red and Assiniboine riverfronts.

Peguis is mentioned in many histories of the area and has been portrayed, for the most part, as a stabilizing influence in the region. He was an early convert to Christianity and a moving spirit in the founding of the Anglican Church at St. Peter's, just below Selkirk.

The book, *Shall We Gather at the River?* by George van der Goes Ladd, presents Peguis as a humane leader and provides an understanding of inter-group relationships in the early nineteenth century. Van der Goes Ladd believes that had Peguis not existed the white man would have had to invent him because Peguis was the "necessary" Indian. The white settlers required a figurehead among the Native people, the writer contends, someone of reasonable stature who could be influenced to follow the white man's line and who would, in turn, influence his own people.

A great deal of this "influencing" was done by the missionaries of the Anglican Church, the first Protestant denomination to send ministers of the Gospel to the Red River. The Anglicans, Van der Goes Ladd writes, set up fourteen parishes along the Red and Assiniboine Rivers. One of these churches was St. Peter's, built by Reverend William Cockran who tried to persuade the Peguis band at Netley Creek to resettle and become farmers.

The Peguis Saulteaux had already been living a partly settled life on their land before the arrival of the Selkirk settlers, tapping maple trees for sugar, growing corn, and occupying more or less fixed habitations. They were different from the Plains Indians who were nomadic and relied largely on the buffalo hunt.

The Selkirk Saulteaux was a relatively small group and may have seen the settlers as useful allies both for support and for information about agriculture. However when the missionaries tried to persuade them to move closer to the church on the east side of the river to build houses and barns there, and to become full-time farmers, many of Peguis' people refused. A major reason for their hesitance lay in their notion of property. The Native view was that land and what it produced should be communally held, and they had great difficulty with the white notion of private property. This and other cultural differences were responsible for many misunderstandings and clashes between whites and Natives right across the west.

Van der Goes Ladd attempts—with limited success—to portray Peguis as a willing ally of the whites. He quotes Peguis' expression of loyalty to Selkirk and to the treaty, words that were recorded by another Anglican missionary, Dr. John West. But Van der Goes Ladd also describes another side of Peguis' character, that which he calls "The Trickster," after one of the chief Native spirit powers called *Nanbozho* or *Wisakedjak*. He writes that Peguis had a strong sense of humour that manifested itself in wry understatement and in appreciation of practical jokes. He cites the treaty with Lord Selkirk in this regard, speculating that Peguis may have signed because it tickled his sense of humour to be regarded as "proprietor of the land thus signed away, land which he had not until then realized he owned."

In 1860 Peguis challenged the Selkirk Treaty in a letter to the *Nor'-Wester* newspaper, in which he questioned the legality of all land claims in the west. In effect, he claimed the Hudson's Bay Company had no right to sell land to Selkirk in the first place—part of which was the subject of the 1817 treaty—since the Natives had never sold or ceded land to the Company. His challenge represented a change of heart, of course, and showed an aspect of Peguis seldom mentioned by historians.

Equally unmentioned by most chroniclers is the fact that Peguis' nickname was "Cut-Nose." Near the end of the 1700s Peguis was involved in a melee at the fur trade post at Pembina. John "Falcon" Tanner, a native of Ohio who was an Indian by adoption, described what he called a "drunken frolic" during the course of which Peguis tried to break up a family quarrel. One of the men involved, not recognizing the would-be peacemaker, grabbed him and bit off his nose. The perpetrator was immediately contrite when he discovered whom he had bitten. Peguis, then in his twenties, passed it of by saying, "I am an old man and it is but a short time they will laugh at me for the loss of my nose."

In fact, he had many more years to live with the disfigurement. Peguis' date of birth is unknown, but Van der Goes Ladd assumes it to be in the mid-1760s or early 1770s. Peguis died in 1864. His family always said he was ninety when he died but, according to Van der Goes Ladd's chronology, he was almost one hundred, a remarkable age for those times.

In his later years, Peguis lost much of the power and prestige he had once enjoyed among his own people. Perhaps his seeming ease with giving in to the settlers and the missionaries weakened him in their eyes. But the old man's heart was still strong on the side of Native tradition. Although some people from Netley did cross the river to St. Peter's, Peguis told Reverend Cockran that the young people of his tribe "would never become slaves to cultivate the ground." And, although he was a convert, Peguis was not baptized until 1838, and only after much inner struggle did he finally agree to the demands of the church and put aside two of his three "wives."

When he died, he was buried at St. Peter's and the anniversary of his death is marked by memorial services. His grave overlooks the stream beside which he lived most of his life, giving fuller meaning to Cockran's description of those Saulteaux who stayed at Netley. "They belong to the river," Cockran wrote.

Pierre the Rhymer

*Pierre Falcon wrote lively songs to commemorate
the events of his day.*

"If I were permitted to write all the ballads I need not care who makes the laws of the land."—Andrew Fletcher

It is unlikely that Pierre Falcon ever heard this quotation. But, for the Métis of the western plains, the quote still describes the man who wrote the songs of the "New Nation." Widely known as Pierriche, or Pierre the Rhymer, he was perhaps the best known of many traditional songmakers among the Métis. The Métis, children of French fathers and Native mothers, were skilled in the ways of the trapline and the buffalo hunt, understood the weather and the secrets of survival, but few were literate. This meant that theirs was an oral culture in which traditions and history had to be committed to memory and handed down verbally from generation to generation.

Pierre Falcon was born at the North West Company's Fort la Coude in the Swan River district on 4 June 1793. His grandfather, also named Pierre, came to Quebec from the Picardy district of France, shortly after the Battle of the Plains of Abraham and the subsequent British takeover of what had been New France.

Grandfather Pierre and his wife, Marie-Geneviève Tremblay, had a son, Pierre Jean Baptiste, for whom the lure of adventure and profit in the west was strong. He entered the service of the North West Company, served as a clerk in the Assiniboine River district, and married a Cree woman with whom he had six daughters and two sons, one of whom was Pierre.

This Pierre was destined to become Pierriche. When he was about five years old he went to Montreal with his father. Although he may have had some schooling there, when he became a songmaker he did not write down his songs but depended on memory, in keeping with Métis oral tradition.

Young Pierre left Montreal in 1807 when he was fourteen to follow in his father's footsteps and joined the North West Company. He worked for a number of years in the Lake of the Woods area and as far west as the Qu'Appelle Valley. During this time, he became a friend of Métis leader Cuthbert Grant. When he was nineteen Falcon married Grant's daughter, Marie, and became closely linked to one of the most outstanding families in the region. Their first few years of marriage would not be peaceful. During those years the rivalry between the North West and Hudson's Bay companies escalated from competition in trade to confrontation and violence.

The Selkirk settlement at the forks of the Red and Assiniboine Rivers was seen by the Nor'Westers and their Métis allies as a deliberate attempt by the HBC to cut off their trade route with Montreal. The animosity deepened when the governor of the Red River Settlement, Miles Macdonell, ordered that no pemmican was to be exported from the region and that the Métis were forbidden to hunt buffalo near the settlement.

The first Métis response to these orders, which threatened their basic way of life, was to carry out isolated acts of harassment against the settlers who were trying to establish themselves as farmers. Then, in 1816, Grant gathered a force of Métis cavalry that included his brother-in-law, Pierre Falcon, and moved toward the main part of the settlement, escorting a shipment of pemmican that had been stolen from an HBC post.

A new governor, Robert Semple, saw the force passing across Frog Plain, west of Fort Douglas, and went out with a body of his men either to find out what the horsemen were doing or to intercept them. The result was the brief and bloody Battle of Seven Oaks in which Semple and nineteen of his men were killed. According to Métis lore, Falcon wrote a song the night after the battle—"*Chanson de la Grenouillere*" ("Ballad of Frog Plain")—that became known along all the Nor'Wester trade routes as the Métis and Québécois voyageurs learned it and sang it everywhere they went.

Lord Selkirk came west from Montreal in 1817 with a force of former soldiers to re-establish his settlement. He captured the North West Company depot at Fort William and arrested senior Nor'Wester officials. There is a story that Falcon was at Fort William when Selkirk arrived there, although whether he was present out of curiosity or on duty is not known.

Another of Falcon's songs from the same period describes a great celebration ball held at Fort William under the patronage of an unnamed English peer (who could only be Lord Selkirk). It closely resembles "*La Grenouillere*" in its satiric style.

The increasing violence between the two fur companies, culminating at Seven Oaks, was followed by the unification of the Nor'Westers and the HBC in 1821. As did many other Métis traders and brigade crews, Falcon obtained employment with the merged companies. However, he soon decided that his family responsibilities were more important than the roving, adventurous life he had been leading. In 1825 he and Marie settled at St. Francois Xavier on the Assiniboine River west of Fort Garry. There, Pierre and Marie brought up three sons and four daughters in a neighbourhood whose inhabitants included Cuthbert Grant and other relatives.

There is strong evidence that Falcon was a very successful farmer, especially in livestock breeding. However, he continued for a time to take part in the buffalo hunt that took place west and south of Red River twice a year. When his sons grew up and married, he split up his original farm to give the young men a start in life.

At least one of his sons, Jean-Baptiste, was active in the buffalo hunt as late as 1851, when Jean-Baptiste was leader of the St. Francois Xavier group that clashed with a large Sioux war party on 14–15 July 1851 at the Battle of the Grand Coteau. During this event, the well-disciplined Métis formed a circle with their carts and successfully stood off repeated Sioux attacks until the raiders gave up and rode off.

Meanwhile, Pierriche continued to make up and sing his songs about subjects of interest to his community. One such song relates the story of James Dickson, an American who had given himself the title of general. "General" Dickson was convinced that he could raise an army with which he would liberate the Native people of Mexico. Dickson had heard of the Métis and thought they would make an excellent cavalry force for his army. He came to St. Francois Xavier and was entertained by Grant, but the Métis weren't interested in Dickson's hare-brained scheme and he rode off into the proverbial sunset. This event made fine material for Falcon. His song, "*Le General Dickson*," allowed him to glorify the Métis people and to poke fun at absurdity.

In 1853 Pierre Falcon was appointed magistrate of the White Horse Plain district surrounding St. Francois Xavier and was known throughout the district as a responsible and highly respected citizen.

> ### *Pierre Falcon and the Census*
> *Appearing at #20 on the 1827 Red River census is:*
> *Pierre Falcon, age 36, Roman Catholic, Rupertsland, 1 married man, 1 woman, 3*
> *sons (-16), 3 daughters (-15), 1 house, 1 stable, 1 mare, 2 cows, 1 calf, 1 swine, 1*
> *cart, 1 canoe, 6 acres, Village of Grant Town or The White Horse Plain.*

Falcon was seventy-six years old when many of the Red River settlers formally resisted the transfer of the Hudson's Bay Company's huge territory to Canadian sovereignty. Although he did not take an active part in the provisional government set up in 1869–70 by Louis Riel and his followers, he did write a song about the rebellion. "*Les Tribulations d'un Roi Malheureux*" ("The Misfortunes of an Unlucky King") described the ill-starred attempt by William McDougall, designated as governor of the North-Western Territory by the government of Canada, to enter the Red River region and proclaim his authority.

The words of some of Falcon's songs were written down by a number of people during his lifetime. According to authorities on the subject, the tunes to which the songs were sung were largely well-known folk songs. Henri Caron and Father Pierre Piston were able to record original tunes to which some of the earlier songs were written.

Some of Falcon's songs contained a refrain repeated after each verse, and most had a very definite beat which lent itself to handclapping accompaniment. Many were admirably suited for use as work songs or accompaniments to canoe paddling. And most of them had a final verse in which Falcon named himself as the author.

The few physical descriptions of Falcon in existence usually include the words "energetic" and "lively." One portrait of him by artist Constantin Tauffenbach depicts him in middle age with a deeply tanned face, hair to his shoulders, penetrating eyes, and a thinly bearded chin.

Falcon died on 28 October 1876 at the age of eighty-three. His wife Marie died the following year. Both were buried in the St. Francois Xavier cemetery.

While there is some controversy over whether Falcon Lake in eastern Manitoba was named for him or for John "Falcon" Tanner, there is no doubt about Pierriche's contribution to Métis culture in Manitoba.

Hiccups and Happiness

John Bunn—doctor, magistrate, and so much more.

Bunn's Creek is a small park-fringed stream that flows from Winnipeg's Lagimodière Boulevard to the Red River, a little south of the Perimeter Highway. Its name commemorates a family that made a considerable contribution to the early development of Winnipeg and Manitoba.

In the year 1800 Napoleon Bonaparte was busy thrashing the Austrians at Marengo, the United States of America was barely twenty-four years old, and the North West Company was racing farther and farther west to try to break the Hudson's Bay Company's 130-year fur trade monopoly. At Moose Factory, the principal HBC trading post on James Bay, Thomas Bunn and his wife Sarah became the parents of a son who was later christened John.

Three years earlier, Thomas Bunn, a tradesman from London, England, had joined the HBC. Sarah Bunn's father was John McNab, a Scottish surgeon who was in charge of the Moose Factory post, and her mother was a member of one of the Native tribes in the area.

In 1803 the Bunn family was transferred to York Factory at the mouth of the Hayes River on Hudson Bay. There, young John and his sister Mary attended a small school. When John was nine his grandfather took him to Scotland, where he lived for the next ten years. He went to school in Edinburgh and, eventually, went to Edinburgh University, where he completed two years of a medical course. Then, to the young student's dismay, Grandfather McNab decided it was time that John returned to Rupert's Land.

In one of his textbooks, John Bunn wrote: "Today, I leave the University for my native country, Hudson Bay. What is before me God knows but I think I am going to the Devil in a cold country, Farewell happiness, farewell my intellectual pleasures . . . In three months, I shall be among a parcel of hairy, frozen devils and think of days never to return."

A few months later, he wrote: "Here I am at Moose Factory . . . A strange pack of uncivilized souls I have got among, to be sure—they speak English, some of them, but I very much wish I were back at 'Auld

Reekie' [Edinburgh]. Goodbye to happiness, where it will end I know not, but a precious kettle of fish my old grandfather has made of it."

Since he had little choice in the matter, Bunn entered the service of the HBC and, in 1821, after the Hudson's Bay and North West Companies amalgamated, was posted to Red River. There, in 1829, he married Catherine Thomas, the daughter of Thomas Thomas, governor of the northern department of Rupert's Land.

John and Catherine had three children. Thomas, the eldest, was to play an active role in the Red River Rebellion of 1869–70. He served as secretary of state in Louis Riel's short-lived provisional government and, later, as a member of the Manitoba Legislature. Thomas Bunn was proud of his mixed blood and declared that if the Dominion surveyors had started their work on English half-breed land, they would have resisted as strongly as did the Métis.

John Bunn was not cut out to be a trader and yearned so much for the profession he had started that, in 1831, he quit the HBC service and returned to Edinburgh for two years. While in Edinburgh he qualified for a licence from the Royal College of Surgeons in anatomy, pharmacy, and surgery. On returning to Red River, Bunn established a practice and was soon in great demand throughout the settlement.

According to letters from the time, John and Catherine were devoted to each other and when she died a few weeks after the birth of their third son, William, John Bunn was deeply affected. Colleagues noted and commented on the strong evidence of bouts of loneliness experienced by Bunn shortly after Catherine's death.

One contemporary described him as "mad—quite mad," but a study of the medical evidence available led a Winnipeg doctor in the 1930s to the opinion that Dr. Bunn was not mad but had at one point suffered a mild stroke that temporarily affected his work and manner and aged him in appearance. His features were such that he had become known throughout the Red River region as "Old Bunn."

He quickly recovered to his former behaviour and threw himself into his medical duties and a wide array of community tasks. He was gregarious by nature and enjoyed those social occasions for which he had time, a commodity in short supply because of his numerous interests.

He was a member of the Council of Assiniboia, which was set up in 1835 after the HBC purchased the settlement from Lord Selkirk's estate, and was a member and later chairman of the public works board, the

The Death of Thomas Simpson

The violent death of Thomas Simpson remains one of the most perplexing mysteries in Manitoba history.

Simpson was a member of the Peter Dease party, which, from 1837 to 1839, conducted three expeditions along the continent's northern coast and much of what was later established as a link to the long-sought-for North-West Passage. In 1840 he came south to Red River, intending to travel to St. Peter's, a Mississippi River trading port, and to proceed from there to England.

Simpson left Fort Garry on 6 June 1840 with a number of traders and Métis but, annoyed by their slow pace, he went ahead with four men. Simpson's small party consisted of Antoine Legros and his son, John Bird (an Englishman), and James Bruce (described as "a Scotch half-breed"). With the smaller party, Simpson moved fast; his diary showed that on 11 June he covered nearly 76 kilometres (47 mi.). But something went dramatically wrong as subsequent investigations revealed that, on either 13 or 14 June, Simpson shot and killed two of his companions, that the surviving two of his party fled on horseback, and that when a group from the main body of travellers reached the location of Simpson's last camp he was either killed or found dead.

According to evidence given by Bruce and young Legros, Simpson began to act in an erratic manner soon after leaving the main party. He rode rapidly ahead of them, then turned back, then dashed off again, urging them to greater speed. When they complained the horses would soon be tired, he insisted on turning back and following an uneven course that, it turned out, placed them in the rear of the main body of travellers with whom he had left Red River.

On 14 June, after changing his mind about where to set up camp, Simpson decided on a spot, gathered all the guns together by his cart, and as Bird and the elder Legros were putting up his tent he shot them both. He then told Bruce and the boy that if they helped him get back to Red River, "the Company will give you five hundred pounds." Instead, the two survivors fled on horseback, found the main party, and led some of them to the scene of the tragedy.

They hailed Simpson, got no reply, but saw him move. Simpson fired a gun, the bullet flying off into the air. Some of the investigators fired back, with one of the shots hitting Simpson's cart and another wounding a dog.

When they finally approached the camp, they found Simpson face down on the ground, his gun under him, its muzzle in line with his head where a bullet had hit him. His body was still warm and "his nightcap [was] blown some yards off, in a line with the position of the gun." As was customary, the party buried Simpson nearby.

News of the event did not get back to Red River until the travellers with whom Simpson had set out returned in October. A group from the colony, including a doctor, later went to the site of the incident, exhumed Simpson's body, and, from what they found, corroborated the evidence given by those who were there at the time.

In his book, The Red River Settlement, *Alexander Ross writes that, while at first there appeared to be some discrepancies in the various accounts, statements from witnesses were enough to indicate that Simpson took his own life, and that the hardships and anxieties experienced on his earlier Arctic explorations had unsettled his mind and driven him to irrational behaviour.*

council's executive group. Bunn was a magistrate from 1837 until his death and was acting recorder, or chief magistrate, from 1858 to 1861. He was also on the finance committee and the committee entrusted with encouraging agriculture and industry. He assisted in writing a report on the status of local laws and legal matters, was governor of the jail, coroner, and, for a time, sheriff of Assiniboia.

The breadth of his interests is illustrated by some of the many subjects on which he made reports and recommendations: the construction of a river road, grants to the Red River Agricultural Association, the appointment of a public surveyor, the importation of a printing press, and several items relating to import duties.

In addition, he was a warden of St. John's Cathedral, the oldest and largest Anglican congregation in the West. In this post he and fellow wardens Alexander Logan and Alexander Ross served so well from 1835 to 1848 that, when they resigned, they could report that they had completely retired the heavy debt that had been incurred by the parish before the three men assumed their duties.

As coroner John Bunn was called on to act in one of the mysteries of the region, the death of Arctic explorer Thomas Simpson, who, with two of his travelling companions, was shot to death on the trail to Pembina (see sidebar, "The Death of Thomas Simpson").

As magistrate, Bunn frequently leavened justice with mercy and was not above uttering humorous comments when warranted. In one case several boatmen were accused of stealing rum from a barrel at a portage between Hudson Bay and Red River. After hearing the evidence, Bunn pronounced an old Scottish verdict: "Not proven." He said this simply meant, "You got off this time, but don't do it again!"

Bunn enjoyed social gatherings, although there is evidence that—along with many other men in this isolated pioneer community—he was inclined to drink too much and suffer the next-day effects. In a letter to a friend in 1848, he described a ball given by the officers of a garrison regiment on the occasion of their departure. "At midnight, there was an elegant spread ... to which ample justice was done. At its close, my memory expired. All became hiccups and happiness."

For years Bunn travelled up and down the length of the settlement, treating and caring for all who needed his services. Fees were never a problem, and he attended many patients who were unable to pay him. The HBC recognized his value to the company by granting him one hundred pounds a year for life. Eden Colville, governor of Rupert's Land in 1851, wrote: "Mr. Bunn is, to my mind, the most sensible man in the settlement, and I do not know how I should have got on without his assistance in the Court and Council."

Most of those who wrote about him showed great appreciation for his work. Mrs. Neil Campbell's memoirs include a recollection of Bunn travelling the river road daily. In summer he was on horseback. In winter he drove his "parchment" cariole, while dressed in a buffalo skin coat and hat and wrapped in a buffalo robe, in which he "was comfortable on even the coldest days."

John Bunn attended his last court session on 21 May 1861. Ten days later he suffered a stroke and died shortly afterward. He was not an earth shaker, but he did much to hold the community together and to provide and protect some of those basic links that distinguish civilization from chaos.

A New People on the Great Plain

Métis scouts employed by the Boundary Commission are an example of the valuable role played by the Métis in the development of the area.

ARCHIVES OF MANITOBA (N14060)

The Métis have played an integral role in Manitoba's history for nearly two centuries, and they remain one of the most misunderstood ethnic groups in Canada.

The word métis comes from the French, originally meaning "mixed"; modern French dictionaries define it as "cross-bred" or "hybrid." The term first came into use in Canada on the Atlantic coast and in what was New France—today's Quebec—as a result of extensive intermarriage between early European settlers and Natives. Leaders of early French settlement, such as Samuel de Champlain, encouraged these unions. "Our young men will marry your daughters and we shall be one people," he is said to have told Native leaders, although there was always the stipulation that these would be church weddings.

Later, as more European women came to the colony, mixed unions were discouraged, and many of the Métis (or *bois-brûlé*) families moved west to the Great Lakes area.

Farther west, in Rupert's Land where the Hudson's Bay Company ruled, resident traders and clerks were ordered not to take what were euphemistically called "country wives." But rules were bent and broken and, by the mid-eighteenth century, the company began to make arrangements for the education of children of "country marriages."

Although the HBC was careful about how far it went in accepting such unions, the children of traders and Indian wives were sometimes referred to as "Natives of Hudson Bay." The words Métis or *bois-brûlé* were scarcely heard in the west until early in the nineteenth century.

Meanwhile, as settlement moved west in the United States and America marked out its northern border in the Great Lakes area, many of the Great Lakes Métis migrated to Manitoba. By the time the first Selkirk settlers arrived in 1812, the Métis and the offspring of Hudson's Bay Company men and Native wives had formed a considerable part of the population of the eastern prairies. Métis men formed the mainstay of the boatmen, wagon drivers, and hunters in the ranks of the North West Company, which rivalled the HBC's trade monopoly as it pushed farther and farther north in search of furs. In addition, the Nor'Westers recruited

Métis men from time to time to form an irregular cavalry force in the continuing struggle between the two fur companies as, for example, at the Battle of Seven Oaks.

But, before that battle led to their merger in 1821, the rival companies had gradually developed different attitudes and policies toward their "country born" allies and employees. HBC officials gave belated support to the Selkirk settlement because they realized Selkirk provided a place where retired company employees could settle with their Native wives and families and remain under the eyes and control of the company. In addition to saving the cost of transporting retirees back to Britain whence most of them came, the HBC could benefit from these residents of the Red River Settlement, spending their pensions and other income in company-controlled trade.

The Nor'Westers, on the other hand, regarded the Métis people with a less paternalistic air, exercising less direct control over them, and, in some cases, regarding them as a distinct ethnic group. One man of high standing in the North West Company councils, William McGillivray, wrote in 1818 that "they one and all look upon themselves as members of an independent tribe of natives, entitled to a property in the soil, to a flag of their own and to protection from the British government." And, he added that they "have formed a separate and distinct tribe of Indians for a considerable time back."

As more former fur trade employees moved to the Red River Settlement with their Native wives and children, the character of the region began to change. One of the changes involved some children of European and Native stock who had been sent back to Britain for education—notably Cuthbert Grant, Métis leader at Seven Oaks, builder of the first water-powered flour mill and, for many years Warden of the Plains, a position with the HBC that involved policing the fur trade, organizing buffalo hunts, and protecting settlements.

Alexander K. Isbister, another of the mixed-race youngsters sent back to be educated in Scotland, wrote in the *Nor'-Wester* newspaper in 1861:

> The half castes or mixed race not only far outnumber all the other races in the colony put together, but engross nearly all the important and intellectual offices—furnishing from their number the sheriff, medical officer, post-master [sic], all the teachers but one, a fair proportion of the magistrates and one of the electors and proprietors of the only newspaper in the Hudson's Bay ter-

ritories. The mixed race . . . are at the moment the dominant class in the country . . . Every married woman and mother of a family throughout the whole extent of the Hudson's Bay territories . . . is (with the exception of small Scottish community at Red River and a few missionaries' wives) of this class and, with her children, the heir to all the wealth of the country.

Isbister and others, including members of the Ross family, were well aware that change was coming in the 1850s and 1860s. Trade had opened up between the Red River and American centres such as St. Paul, as a result of the HBC's grudging admission that it could no longer exercise or enforce its former monopolistic control over the entire fabric of life in Rupert's Land.

The HBC monopoly in the West had been challenged and questioned for some decades before 1870, and the Hind and Palliser expeditions to the prairies aroused great interest among adventurous and entrepreneurial people in Ontario, Britain, and some parts of the United States. Many Ontarians felt that their province should be extended west to take in the Red River among other areas. This idea was strongly opposed by Quebecers, who felt their influence in the country would be weakened.

There seemed to be three possible futures for the Red River Settlement at the time. It could have been: annexed by Ontario, made into a crown colony by Britain (as had taken place on the Pacific coast), or annexed by the United States, as was strongly urged by the Minnesota state legislature in 1862. By the late 1860s, however, final negotiations were underway to buy out the HBC rights in the North-West, and the government of Canada sent out surveyors to map the Red and Assiniboine River valleys.

It was the arrival of these surveyors that sparked the movement led by Métis leader Louis Riel that ultimately brought about the formation of the province of Manitoba and its entry into Confederation. The controversy about Louis Riel's role in the events of 1869–70 is still alive in some quarters, but he and his colleagues unquestionably created the occasion for calling Manitoba into being.

With the influx of settlers in the late 1800s, the Métis became an increasingly smaller component of the population and less influential in the affairs of the region. However, it must be remembered that they were, at one time, the new people on the plain, predominant in all aspects of life in what is now Manitoba and, in fact, western Canada.

Two Worlds Shaped His Life

This medicine chest belonged to Cuthbert Grant,
one of the powerful men of the early 1880s.

North of the Portage Avenue bridge over Sturgeon Creek in Winnipeg stands a working replica of an old-fashioned gristmill. It commemorates the efforts of Métis leader, Cuthbert Grant, to improve his people's condition. The location of the original 1829 water mill built by Grant is not known, but Winnipeg's replica represents an innovative experiment by a man whose name has virtually slipped into oblivion.

From 1812 to 1849 Cuthbert Grant was an influence to be reckoned with by the fur trade companies, by the Selkirk settlers, and by the Métis and Natives of the plains region. Grant had charisma, that hard-to-define quality that gives its possessors the power to influence and lead others. In this respect, Grant stands alongside men like Louis Riel, George Simpson, John Diefenbaker, and Pierre Trudeau who, whatever one's personal opinion of them may be, made tremendous impacts on the future of our country and on the minds of their fellow Canadians.

Cuthbert Grant was born in 1793 at a North West Company trading post called Fort Tremblants in the upper reaches of the Assiniboine River Valley. His father, also named Cuthbert, was a trader who had carried the Nor'Wester flag far into the north, helped establish Fort Resolution, and met Alexander Mackenzie on his epic voyage to the Arctic Ocean down the river bearing his name.

Cuthbert Grant Senior came from Scotland and, at some point, took a "country wife" whose name is unknown, but who was likely half-European and half-Cree. Cuthbert Grant Junior was one of five children. After his father's death in 1799, young Cuthbert, like his elder brother James before him, was sent to Montreal where he was baptized in the Scotch Presbyterian Church in 1801 and then, according to family and company tradition, sent to Scotland to go to school.

Cuthbert later returned to Canada and a position in the North West Company headquarters in Montreal to learn the fur trade. He was sent west in 1812. On the way he visited the company's Fort Gibraltar (Fort Garry's predecessor) where his brother-in-law was in charge of the trading post. Cuthbert was then sent to a post on the Qu'Appelle River. He became a close friend of John Richards McKay, the Hudson's Bay Company post manager at Brandon House, and took McKay's sister, Bethsy, as his wife in a "country marriage." She bore a son in 1814.

Meanwhile, the Selkirk settlers were moving into the Red River Valley. The North West Company opposed this project for two reasons: they rejected the HBC claim to sovereignty over Rupert's Land; and they charged that until the settlers were established their need for a share of the food supplies of the country—mainly pemmican—would cut sharply into the requirements of the fur traders on their long voyages to the West.

The North West Company had been, to a considerable degree, father and mother to Cuthbert Grant, and his loyalty to the company was reinforced by his renewed sense of belonging to the life of the western plains. He had rapidly become a figure of some importance and influence among the young Métis in the area between the Red River and what is now Saskatchewan, and the company used this influence to spearhead its campaign to drive out the Selkirk settlers.

From 1814 to 1816 a series of events heightened the hostility between settlers and Nor'Westers. First, the Selkirk settlers' governor, Miles Macdonell, ordered that buffalo hunting near the settlement should stop because the Métis method of hunting drove the herds farther west, out of reach of the colonists. The Métis rejected Macdonell's order and put forward their claim that they were a new nation and that this was their land.

Grant was chosen as captain of the Métis. His background, mastery of Métis skills, and personality drew the Métis to him and generated a wide measure of respect for him. While senior Nor'Wester partners were urging the Métis to flout the buffalo hunting ban, they were also trying to persuade the individual settlers to leave the colony for the safer prospects of farm life in Upper Canada.

They cajoled some forty settlers into leaving. At the same time, the Nor'Westers and Métis conducted a campaign of harassment against the settlers who had decided to stay. In June 1814 muskets and cannon were used to repel a Métis attack on Fort Douglas (where Winnipeg's Point Douglas is now), farmers were repeatedly intimidated while at work, and cattle were driven off. The Métis arrested Macdonell, torched cabins, and presided over a small reign of terror, which was alleviated only by the services of Chief Peguis, long a friend of the settlers.

The state of unrest continued as new groups of settlers arrived from Britain and culminated in the Battle of Seven Oaks on 19 July 1816, when Grant and his Métis cavalry defeated the Selkirk settlement's governor, Robert Semple, killing him and most of his small band.

Grant surrendered after being served a warrant charging him with culpability for the Seven Oaks episode and for the murder of Owen Keveny, a settler who was shot en route to Montreal. Grant went to Montreal, where a grand jury failed to bring a charge against him, and he returned to the West.

On his return to the Qu'Appelle Valley in 1818, Grant was a changed man. He realized he had been used by the North West Company. As a result, when the North West and Hudson's Bay Companies were forcibly united in 1821, he took service with the HBC.

An additional cause for Grant's change in character may have been that, when he returned, he found his wife, Bethsy, and their son had disappeared, leaving no trace of what had happened to them.

Grant was a troubleshooter for the HBC, helping wherever there was a problem with Indians or Métis, in free trading, and in the organization of supply boat trips to Norway House. In 1828 he was named Warden of the Red River Plains by the HBC, with a salary of two hundred pounds a year, and obtained a considerable acreage near the White Horse Plains where he settled a number of Métis families. In this semi-agricultural enclave, then named Grantown and now called St. Francois Xavier, he ruled for a time in the manner of a grand seigneur. He was a member of the Council of Assiniboia, the administrative body appointed by the HBC, and was well known both to the Red River Colony and to visitors.

He tried to improve the lot of the Grantown people by building a water-powered mill on Sturgeon Creek. This failed but Grant did replace it with several windmills, which continued to provide service to his people for a number of years.

By 1849 Grant's influence was on the decline. In that year a free-trader named William Sayer was arrested and brought to trial for breaking the HBC monopoly. The proceedings were brief, mostly because a large crowd of armed Métis, against Grant's advice, surrounded the courthouse and entered the courtroom. Their hostile manner produced a guilty verdict without a penalty being applied. This was greeted by the assembled Métis with cries of: "*Le commerce est libre!* Trade is free!"

Grant's last years were marred by increased drinking. In a society where heavy alcohol consumption was the norm, his drinking was seen as excessive. He was buried in 1854 the Grantown churchyard.

The Little Emperor

*George Simpson, who oversaw the HBC with an
iron hand, is seen on an inspection trip,
complete with piper.*

ARCHIVES OF MANITOBA (N10897)

He was called the "Little Emperor" by many of his fur trade colleagues because of his manner and methods, not as a sign of affection.

George Simpson entered the service of the Hudson's Bay Company at a time when great changes were taking place in the fur trade. The long and often violent conflict between the 150-year-old HBC and the much younger North West Company had ended with the merger of the two in 1821.

Simpson was the illegitimate son of George Simpson Senior and a woman whose name is not recorded. His birthdate is also uncertain but was most likely in 1786 or 1787. His grandfather, Reverend Thomas Simpson, was minister of Avioch, a Highland Scottish parish.

Young George learned reading, grammar, arithmetic, and geography in the Avioch parish school. At the age of thirteen or fourteen, he went to London with his uncle, Geddes Simpson, whose company was in the sugar trade with the West Indies. Shortly after that, Geddes went into partnership with Andrew Wedderburn-Colville, whose sister Elizabeth was the wife of Thomas Douglas, the fifth Earl of Selkirk.

Wedderburn-Colville and Lord Selkirk became major stakeholders in the Hudson's Bay Company in order to assist Selkirk's plans to resettle evicted crofters from northern Scotland on a grant of land at the junction of the Red and Assiniboine Rivers.

Wedderburn-Colville was so impressed by young George Simpson's grasp of business affairs and his apparent future as a mover and shaker that he arranged for Simpson to be hired by the HBC and sent out to Rupert's Land.

At that time, the company's two senior officers in Rupert's Land were Colin Robertson, who was waging a campaign to break the Nor'Westers' firm hold on the Athabasca region trade, and William Williams, the governor of the territory. The HBC felt that Robertson was spending far too much money on his task. In addition, he had been forced to declare personal bankruptcy. In 1818 Williams had distinguished himself by putting guns on a schooner, sailing it on Lake Winnipeg to Grand Rapids, and capturing the Nor'Westers' Athabasca fur brigade with its entire cargo of furs. However, with the merger of the two companies being negotiated and strict ordinances from the British government that all violence in the fur trade must cease, both Robertson and Williams were felt to be yesterday's men.

George Simpson, age thirty-four, with little knowledge of either North America or the fur trade, was pitchforked into the tangled task of reconciling the former enemies and reorganizing an enterprise that stretched from Montreal to the Rocky Mountains, from the uncertain boundary with the United States to the Arctic.

Many of those employed by the two companies were uncertain about their futures. Morale was low, and there were far too many people and trading posts for what was, in effect, a total monopoly of the trade. The Nor'Westers' equipment, such as canoes and post buildings, was better, while the HBC had somewhat superior trade goods.

Simpson's first task was to meet the Nor'Wester partners at Fort William (now Thunder Bay, Ontario) to tell them how things were going to be under the new regime. At the meeting he learned that Robertson had been captured by the rival company and that Williams, as senior man, was appointing him as Robertson's replacement in the Athabasca.

Simpson made a fast trip to the region where, at the main HBC post on Lake Athabasca, he found a tense situation between the employees of the two companies. With a display of personal bravery and the use of a good deal of bluffing, he defused the tension, laying the foundation for his reputation for toughness and quick decision making that was to become widely known during much of his later career.

Early in his career Simpson dedicated himself to the service of his employers and displayed a willingness to use any means to increase their influence and enhance their profits. In a relatively short time, using whatever means suited the immediate occasion (harshness, flattery, or inspiration), he began to bring about the complete reorganization of the HBC's fur trade, which was to make his name and his reputation known throughout the land.

When the union of the HBC and the North West Company was finally completed in 1821, Williams became governor of the southern department—the James Bay area and posts in Canada and along the American border—while Simpson was named governor of the northern department. His region was vast, taking in most of the former Rupert's Land and the entire Pacific coast.

Simpson's methods of dealing with many of the enlarged company's problems were short, sharp, and very much to the point. He identified the posts that were to be declared redundant and the employees whose contracts were to be terminated. Clerks, tradesmen, and other employees who were no longer needed were paid what was owed them and given passage back to wherever they came from, be it Britain, or Upper or Lower Canada.

Simpson also felt pay rates were too high. He waited until midwinter before announcing sizable reductions in wage scales. Anyone who would not accept the new terms would have to leave the posts where they were employed. The result was exactly what Simpson had in mind. Travel was difficult, if not impossible, in winter, and besides, there were no other employers in that vast land to which disgruntled workers could go for jobs. The new pay rates were grudgingly accepted, and, over the next few years, HBC profits showed a large and welcome increase.

Through the results he obtained and by frequent displays of his total devotion to the company's interests, Simpson became head of all HBC operations in North America. He maintained and consolidated his position by tirelessly travelling the territory for which he was responsible and by showing up suddenly, always with a great display of pomp and ceremony, at the various establishments in his vast domain.

He could be, depending on circumstances and the needs of the occasion, persuasive and charming, or curt and cruel. When, as a young man in the first few years of his governorship, he felt the need for female company, he took "country wives" from among the Natives of the land. But, from the tone of his recorded remarks and of mentions in his and others' letters, he had little regard for his temporary partners as human beings.

In an 1822 letter, he wrote: "I suspect my name will become as notorious as the late Gov. [Williams] in regard to plurality of wives." He referred to one of his Native mistresses as "my article" and "my Japan helpmate." In another letter, he instructed his close friend and associate John George McTavish: "If you can dispose of the Lady it will be satisfactory as she is an unnecessary & expensive appendage."

In 1830, when he was in his mid-forties, Simpson married his cousin, Frances Simpson, who was described as "a beautiful young woman of almost eighteen." For the new Mrs. Simpson, the voyage to New York was an ordeal. Several weeks on a sailing ship was no luxury cruise at the best of times, and she suffered greatly from seasickness.

A second gruelling experience for her came with the several weeks of canoe travel from Montreal to Red River, during which the party set up camp for the night anywhere between seven and midnight and were on the water again by three or four in the morning. However, some of the hardship was eased by the fact that, as John S. Galbraith wrote in his biography of Simpson, *The Little Emperor:* "The progress from post to post was in the nature of a royal procession, with the officers outdoing themselves in efforts to do honor to the governor and his new wife, and to show what gentility they were capable of mustering."

To accommodate his new wife, Simpson built a large stone house within the walls of Lower Fort Garry where the Simpsons occasionally entertained. Company was severely limited by Simpson's wish to separate himself from his previous relationships with Native women and by Frances's unwillingness to have anything to do with Native or mixed-race women except on an employer-servant basis.

Frances had a difficult pregnancy in 1831 but both parents were delighted when she bore a son named George Geddes. Sadly, the child died suddenly in 1832.

Simpson realized that life in a frontier settlement was too much for his wife's health, so he persuaded the HBC to buy them a house in Lachine, just outside Montreal. Frances and their four children lived in Lachine for several years, although the children went to school in England, and Frances herself made several trips to London.

On his own frequent trips to England, Simpson was involved in matters other than company business. As an acknowledged expert on the country, he was called for consultation in the long and complicated disputes between Britain and the United States over the boundary between the United States and what would later be Canada. For this, and for other services in consolidating British influence in the West, Simpson received a knighthood in 1841 and afterward was always referred to as Sir George.

Although Sir George drove everyone connected with him to the limits of their ability, he was just as hard on himself. On several occasions he suffered from intestinal disorders and impaired vision that forced him to take complete rest for several weeks. When he was well, however, he set a pace few could keep up with, both in travelling and in handling business.

As he grew older, Simpson limited his travelling through the fur trade country, spending more of his time in Montreal where he became involved in the railroad-building enterprises that marked the 1840s and 1850s. By then the great days of the fur trade were over. Settlers began to push into the territory that became the state of Minnesota. By 1860 the state had a population of one hundred seventy thousand, making it a giant compared to the Red River Settlement.

Frances Simpson died in 1853, and for a time Sir George was depressed. But he rallied his strength and was able to take part in the complex negotiations aimed at resolving the problem of what should be done with the vast HBC territories. He was active during the 1860 visit of the Prince of Wales (later King Edward VII), but his strenuous efforts on behalf of the company over the years and his successive illnesses finally brought him down.

He died at his house in Lachine on 7 September 1860 and was buried beside Frances in Mount Royal Cemetery. The estate he left, worth more than a hundred thousand pounds (likely about a million dollars today), was an indication of his business skill and ability.

"Simpson's death," wrote Galbraith, "marked the passing not only of a man but of a phase in North American history . . . He arrived on the scene when unrestrained competition was giving way to unchallenged monopoly. His attributes were perfectly attuned to govern the amalgamated Company. By guile and firmness, he reconciled old rivals to cooperation. He ruthlessly eliminated waste and promoted efficiency . . . Such a man could not have appeared prior to 1820 and could not emerge after 1860. The times gave him the opportunity for greatness; he capitalized magnificently on the opportunity."

Old Soldiers Never Die, They Go to Manitoba

Fort Douglas as it appeared at the time of its recapture from the North West Company on 10 January 1817.

The name de Meurons made its first appearance in Manitoba after the bloody Battle of Seven Oaks in June 1816. It soon went on to become one of the best known—and controversial—names in the early history of the region. But even before the de Meurons took part in one of the turning points in the development of Canada, they had already enjoyed a colourful history.

News of the Seven Oaks incident and of the forcible removal of the farmer-settlers along the Red River by the North West Company's forces had quickly reached Montreal and the man who had inspired the settlement—Lord Selkirk. Selkirk immediately engaged about one hundred officers and men of the disbanded de Meurons and de Wattville regiments who were, for the most part, at loose ends in Lower Canada, and dispatched them to the West.

The de Meurons regiment, named for a former commander of the regiment, originated in Europe. It was composed of a strange mixture of nationalities, as were many of the regiments involved in the Napoleonic Wars—French, German, Polish, and Italians—but the majority were from the German parts of Switzerland. Some had fought in the War of 1812 and many had seen active service in Ceylon (now Sri Lanka) as well as in European campaigns. They were mercenary soldiers, and, like most of their kind, they were competent in their trade but had little experience with—or desire for—the gentler arts of peacetime living.

By the time Lord Selkirk needed their services, Napoleon had been tucked safely away in exile on St. Helena and the market for old soldiers was less than promising.

Alexander Ross, one of the earliest historians of the Red River Settlement, described them as "with exceptions a rough and lawless set of blackguards." The terms of their agreement with Lord Selkirk included a fixed amount of pay per month for moving boats and canoes from Montreal to Red River using the old North West Company route. In addition, after they had reclaimed the settlement, they were offered grants of land. However, if they decided not to take the land grants, they could demand to return either to Montreal or to Europe at Lord Selkirk's expense.

Not all of the ex-soldiers of the de Meurons and de Wattville regiments in Montreal were hired by Selkirk. Several of them joined the ranks of the North West Company, active opponents of the Red River Settlement. Considering their lives as mercenaries and their temperaments as hired fighters, it is little wonder they were attracted to a life in the hinterland that appeared to offer them further opportunities for a restless and adventurous time.

Take Charles de Reinhard, for example. He had been a colour-sergeant in the de Meurons unit and, in 1816 as a special constable of the Nor'Westers, he was involved in the arrest and murder of Owen Keveny, a leader of the Selkirk settlement. Reinhard and several others were arrested for this murder, and Reinhard saved his own skin by turning King's evidence at the trial (see sidebar, "The Murder of Owen Keveny").

Another former member of the de Meurons who joined the Nor'Westers was Frederick Damien Heurter, who was a member of Cuthbert Grant's Métis force, which advanced eastward along the Assiniboine River in a bid to recapture Fort Douglas in January 1817. Heurter recalled, in a narrative written later, that when Grant received a copy of a Royal proclamation ordering everyone in "Indian country" to keep the peace, Grant threw the proclamation in the fire with the exclamation, "*Voilà encore une autre des sacre proclamations!*" ("Here's another of those damned proclamations!")

The de Meurons and de Wattville men in Lord Selkirk's pay were under the command of a former officer of the de Meurons, Captain Protais D'Orsonnens. With Miles Macdonell, a survivor of the Seven Oaks battle, he led a body of soldiers up the Great Lakes to capture the North West Company headquarters at Fort William in 1816. This expedition then moved west to Rainy Lake and reached the Red River via the Savanne Portage and Roseau River. Their guide was John "Falcon" Tanner.

On arrival at the Red River, the D'Orsonnens-Macdonell force captured the North West Company fort at Pembina on 3 December 1816 and marched down the Red River toward the Forks. In bitterly cold weather, they arrived at Fort Douglas, held by the Nor'Westers, and, in the dark hours of 10 January 1817, they surrounded the fort. North West Company commander Archibald McLellan had only fifteen men in his garrison and surrendered without firing a shot.

The recapture of Fort Douglas meant that the Selkirk settlers, who

The Murder of Owen Keveny

Who was Owen Keveny, and why was he killed by his rescuers on the long canoe trip between the Winnipeg River and Rainy Lake in 1816?

Keveny, an employee of the Hudson's Bay Company, led a party of Selkirk settlers who reached Red River in 1812. After the Battle of Seven Oaks in 1816, when the colony was dispersed by the Nor'Westers, Keveny was sent to help restore it. En route to the settlement, some members of his party deserted and defected to the North West Company at its Bas de la Rivière post, at the mouth of the Winnipeg River.

At Bas de la Rivière Keveny's remaining party was held by Archibald Norman MacLeod, who was empowered to act as magistrate for the Indian Territory. He questioned those remaining loyal to Keveny and issued a warrant for Keveny's arrest.

One of the Nor'Westers at Bas de la Rivière was Charles de Reinhard, who had been a colour-sergeant in the de Meurons regiment, a body of European mercenaries. De Reinhard and one of those who deserted from Keveny's party—Thomas Costello—were appointed constables and arrested Keveny. The day after his arrest, Keveny was sent under guard to Fort William. Near Lake of the Woods, however, the party halted on hearing that Lord Selkirk and a force of former de Meurons had seized the fort.

Keveny's guards, quarrelling over a shortage of provisions, abandoned him on a small island. When they returned to Bas de la Rivière, Nor'Wester Archibald McLellan, who was in charge of the area, went south to see if he could find out what Selkirk's plans were and also to find Keveny. Cuthbert Grant was in McLellan's party.

McLellan rescued Keveny and treated him well but, once again, held him as a prisoner. He was sent ahead of the McLellan party with de Reinhard, an Indian named Joseph, and the Métis Mainville as guards.

They had not gone far when, at a stop along the way, Mainville shot Keveny who was then stabbed by de Reinhard. It is uncertain if McLellan had hinted broadly that he would not mind if the HBC man met with an "accident" en route.

However, de Reinhard, for reasons known only to him, confessed to the murder and stood trial in Montreal, where he turned Crown's witness at the trials of Grant, McLellan, and several other Nor'Westers, who were charged with the murders of Seven Oaks colony leader Robert Semple as well as Keveny.

A grand jury ordered McLellan and de Reinhard to face trial for the Keveny murder, but Grant was cleared. McLellan and de Reinhard were transferred to Upper Canada, and, after the trials, de Reinhard won his freedom in exchange for his evidence.

Why was Keveny murdered? There is nothing to suggest that he had personal enemies or that he had done anything to incur the enmity of those who were guarding him. It appears he was just another victim of the rivalry between the fur trading companies whose competition became so costly in goods and lives that they were forced to amalgamate a few years later.

had fled to Jack River on Lake Winnipeg after Seven Oaks, could return to their homes.

Meanwhile, early in June 1817, Lord Selkirk, with another force of de Meurons and British soldiers, was reported to be on his way west. The Nor'Westers wanted to ensure their supply route past the Forks and down to the Winnipeg River, and to assist in this, Cuthbert Grant led a strong party of Métis east along the Assiniboine. William Laidlaw, Louis Nolin, and Heurter (who had changed sides again), led a body of men from Fort Douglas in an attempt to arrest Grant. Although he served the arrest warrant, Laidlaw was unable to lay hands on Grant, whose men seized their weapons. Grant finally agreed to surrender the next day, but failed to show up.

After Lord Selkirk's arrival on 21 June, Grant once again tried to force a passage for the North West Company supplies but failed to do so when his followers, deterred by the presence of the de Meurons and the British, refused to fight.

This was the last effort by the Métis under Grant to impose the will of the North West Company on the settlement. Many of the de Meurons accepted land grants from Selkirk and were located on small holdings around the mouth of the Seine River where it enters the Red.

In 1819, a welcome opportunity for some of the de Meurons showed itself when William Williams, the Hudson's Bay Company governor, decided the time had come to strike a hard blow at the Nor'Westers. He recruited a company of the ex-soldiers, outfitted and armed a schooner, and set out down Lake Winnipeg on an expedition that he believed would halt the Nor'Westers.

He was successful in ambushing and capturing the North West Company fur brigade coming down the Saskatchewan River at Grand Rapids, although he was himself later captured by the Nor'Westers. Peace had now been established between the Nor'Westers and the settlers, but following the years of strife, the great flood of 1826 was the last straw for many of the recent arrivals, military and civilian alike. As soon as it was possible to do so, most of the Swiss immigrants and the remnants of the de Meurons and de Wattville soldiers departed south. Many of them settled on the upper Mississippi River where some of their descendents still live.

Enforcing Law and
Order in Red River

*Two young men were arrested in Winnipeg
for murder, in 1918.*

Maintaining and enforcing law and order in the Red River Valley was a difficult and dangerous business in the decades before there was such as thing as municipal police services or the RCMP.

In the valley, where the land was under the Hudson's Bay Company's thumb for two hundred years, the company gradually assumed the responsibility and the authority for maintenance of order. In 1833 the company created the Council of Assiniboia, an appointed body that set up a relatively simple framework of laws and levied certain taxes and duties on such things as imports to finance, at least in part, the administration of its rules. Although the HBC appointed individuals to enforce such rules and laws as there were, there were complaints from time to time about the lack of law enforcement.

The first sheriff of Assiniboia, John Spencer, took office in 1816. Two constables were named in 1823, and one Justice of the Peace heard any cases that arose. In 1834 the HBC took over the governance of Lord Selkirk's settlement, increased the number of Justices of the Peace to four, and added a recorder in the person of Adam Thom.

Andrew Bulger, who was appointed governor in 1822, was particularly critical of the colonists. "What can be expected," he wrote, "of dishonest paupers such as the great majority of the settlers are, when there is no jail, no magistrate and no power to restrain their evil propensities?"

Things weren't much improved by the arrival in 1848 of 140 Chelsea Pensioners—old or disabled soldiers who came, many with their families, as a possible law-enforcement body. Some of them quickly gained the censure of the settlers for their drinking habits and disregard for the law. Their commander, Major W. B. Caldwell, was also appointed governor of Assiniboia, but his term of office was largely ineffective since he quickly realized his men were no match for the Métis "cavalry" of the buffalo hunt.

It was on Caldwell's watch that the infamous Sayer trial took place. Guillaume Sayer was charged with infringing on the HBC trade monopoly. A great crowd of armed Métis surrounded the courthouse and so intimidated everyone that the court finally found him guilty, but refused to impose a penalty. The Métis and those demanding free trade in furs were jubilant. From that day forward, the HBC's monopoly existed only in name.

On two occasions troops were sent from England to protect the settlement from real or fancied dangers as a result of the actions of the American government. From 1846 to 1848, more than three hundred members of the 6th Royal Regiment of Foot (Warwickshires) were stationed in the Red River Valley. By all accounts, they were successful in providing a steadying influence and in letting the United States know that Britain was paying attention to events along the border and in the Oregon Territory.

The second garrison was brought in at the request of Governor George Simpson when the United States Army established garrisons of its own in the northern Dakotas and in Minnesota, and when the Métis fur traders showed signs of drifting under American influence. A strong detachment of the green-uniformed Royal Canadian Rifles arrived in 1857 and stayed until 1861.

Historian W. L. Morton noted that "the presence of the green-coated Canadian Rifles at Fort Garry quieted the turbulent spirits in the colony, but when the time for relief came in 1861, the Company declined to assume the cost of paying replacements and the War Office to maintain troops in a location so isolated."

The next upheaval in the settlement requiring the dispatch of troops to the area was the Red River Rebellion of 1869–70, when Métis leader Louis Riel established a short-lived provisional government that lasted only until the arrival of Colonel Garnet Wolseley's Red River Expedition. By that time, the province of Manitoba had been created, and the troops remained only long enough to ensure that the fledgling civil authority was established. This was no small task, considering that the area had only a short time earlier been deemed to be in a state of rebellion.

A mounted detachment of the Quebec Rifles under the command of Captain Frank Villiers was formed in 1870 and had their work cut out for them. Hostility between the so-called Canadian Party led by Dr. John Schultz and former Riel supporters frequently broke out in violent action, and the peace was severely tested during the federal election of 1872.

At the opening of the polling booths in St. Boniface, the two hostile groups went after each other with guns and clubs. Some of the troops were ordered to protect the polls in Winnipeg, and Villiers and some of his company were injured in the fracas. Members of the mob closed the day's frenzied activity with attacks on the three newspaper offices then in operation. They destroyed papers, smashed up the presses, and scattered the type before order was restored.

The new province's government was placed in the hands of an elected Legislative Assembly and, for a short time, a sort of provincial senate. In a few years the Legislative Assembly created the City of Winnipeg, which required an elected city council and a body of bylaws to govern the relationships between its citizens and staff.

The Winnipeg Police Force was created in January 1874, with Chief J. S. Ingram and two constables, William Bruce and D. B. Murray. This small group was faced with a large task as the population of the new city quickly reached five thousand. It was a boom town, attracting a wide variety of adventurers, speculators, gamblers, and prostitutes, mainly from the south and east.

The Manitoba Free Press editorialized on the topic: "The frontier towns of Minnesota and Dakota have poured out a good many of their vile characters into Winnipeg. The spectacles of flashy women driving through the streets from one saloon to another are not conducive to good morals and the fair reputation of the city."

Chief Ingram was not the right man to restore Winnipeg's good name. He was referred to by a writer of the time as "perhaps the greatest rowdy in Winnipeg. Under the cloak of his authority, he engaged in all kinds of dissipation." But not for long.

Stung, perhaps, by the harsh comments from both local and national critics, Ingram's senior constable, D. B. Murray, swooped down one night on a notorious brothel in the western part of the city. One of the "found-ins," as they were called, was Chief Ingram. Murray arrested him and locked him up in the city jail.

City council acted with commendable speed, accepting Ingram's resignation and appointing Murray as the new chief of police, a position he held until 1875. Under Murray's conscientious command, many of Winnipeg's illicit drinking places, gambling establishments, and houses of prostitution were closed—or at least were driven so far under cover that they were no longer exposed to the indignant stare of the law-abiding citizenry.

Since then, Winnipeg has had its share of crime—robberies, assaults, and cases of the more genteel, but still costly, activity known as white-collar crime. Parimutuel betting at the city's racetracks cut into the business of bookies and other gambling establishments and, more recently, lotteries and casinos have made previously illegal activities respectable and productive of revenue for the government. Prostitution is still with us, and every year private disagreements and animosities produce a crop of murder investigations and trials.

But, by and large, the city has been fortunate in its varied police forces. With cruiser cars, radio, and all the advanced paraphernalia of today, police forces are far different from those of its past. There was a time when most policemen in Winnipeg were large burly Scotsmen, formidable enough in summer, but even more so in winter when their buffalo hide coats and hats made them look larger than life as they patrolled the streets.

A Return to Noah's Adventure

*A CBC announcer (believed to be Marsh Phimister)
views the 1950 flood for radio broadcast.*

ARCHIVES OF MANITOBA (N13364)

The "Flood of the Century," which devastated parts of Manitoba along the Red River in 1997, was not the first time that residents of the valley have had to battle Mother Nature. In fact, the Red River basin has a long history of periodic flooding. Native oral history and the recorded observations of such explorer-traders as Nolin, Henry, and Kelsey mention floods as far back as 1776. The rivers rose to varying heights in 1790, 1809, 1815, 1826, and 1852—the three latter dates were marked by losses and privation among the first settlers. Major floods occurred in 1892, 1904, 1916, 1948, 1950, 1966, 1974, 1979, 1993, and, of course, 1997.

The early Selkirk settlers had only been in the area for two or three years when the 1815 flood happened, and although the damage was severe, the devastation of later floods increased in proportion to the increase in settlement and development.

One of the most vivid accounts of the flood of 1826 is that given by Alexander Ross in his book, *The Red River Settlement, its Rise, Progress and Present State*. Written in 1856, the book is a record of Ross's personal experiences of the flood. He had come to Red River in 1825 after a short period teaching in Ontario and fur trading on the West Coast.

The summer of 1825, he wrote, was very wet. "The country was thoroughly saturated; the lakes, swamps and rivers at the fall of the year were full of water and a large quantity of snow had fallen during the preceding winter [1825–26]." A late spring, a sudden surge of warm weather, and days of south winds quickly melted the snow, but ice from the United States rushed down the Red River to Lake Winnipeg where the lake ice blocked it. This blockage sent the meltwater spilling over the river's banks in all directions.

Ross wrote that the water rose nearly 3 metres (10 ft.) in twenty-four hours, which surprised even the Cree and Ojibway who were present on that warm 2 May. By 5 May, the entire settlement had been abandoned.

Ross wrote: "At this crisis, every description of property became of secondary consideration . . . The people had to fly from their homes for their dear life, some saving only the clothes they had on their backs. The shrieks of children, lowing of cattle and barking of dogs added terror to the scene." Fortunately, a number of Hudson's Bay Company employees moved everyone to higher ground and safety, while livestock were driven several miles to dry land.

Where boats were available, many settlers returned to their water-encircled houses. Some had to break through the roofs to rescue seed grain and necessary utensils. As the current grew stronger, everything was swept away, and Ross described "the most singular spectacle, a house in flames, drifting along in the night, one half immersed in water and the remainder furiously burning."

By 21 May, the water had started to recede, and people began returning to their plots of land, even those who had been seriously discussing the relocation of the colony. Ross was among those who lost everything and who finally found refuge for several weeks on the banks of Sturgeon Creek.

As a result of the flood, some of the Swiss and de Meurons members of the community decided to leave; more than two hundred of them left on 24 June for the United States, where many of them settled along the Mississippi.

The Scottish settlers, however, began immediately to rebuild, plow, and plant. Their energy and skill was so great that they had new houses by fall and a small crop of potatoes, barley, and even a little wheat. By 1830 Ross reported that 204 new houses had been erected, as well as fences, barns, and storage sheds. The saturation of the soil, he added, produced good crops for several years.

It would be twenty-six years before anything close to the flood of 1826 took place. The river levels began to rise again late in April 1852. An interesting point is that in the 1826 and 1852 floods, the crest was reached on the same date, 22 May. The water started to recede on 21 May in the flood of 1950.

In 1852 one of the settlers wrote: "Houses and barns were floating in all directions like sloops under sail, with dogs and poultry in them . . . The very mice, snakes and squirrels could not find a safe place."

In the Red River Valley, the waters rise gradually, one might almost say insidiously. Since the valley is so wide, there is never a wall of water rushing with destructive force as happens in some parts of the world. Perhaps that is why only two lives have been lost in Winnipeg's floods prior to 1997—one in 1826 and one in 1950.

Campbell's Ark

One Red River family, the Campbells, managed to get through the flood of 1852 in relative comfort, thanks to the keen eye and resourcefulness of their grandfather.

Grandfather Campbell was sure there were going to be some unpleasant circumstances following a winter of heavy snow. He warned the younger members of his family but they were not concerned. Grandfather, however, quickly formed a plan and put it into action.

He selected the highest ground on his son's farm and began to build a stout framework between four large trees. As soon as the water began to rise, the rest of the family suddenly found Grandfather's idea a very good one, and ten relatives arrived to help finish the framing, siding, and caulking of what looked rather like a house, but was, in fact, an ark.

By the time the flood had risen to the point where the Campbell houseboat started floating, everyone was aboard, and their ship of refuge was strongly tied to the trees around it. They had stored all they needed, including seed grain, clothing, and pemmican and other dried food. Using their homemade dugout canoes, they were able to bring in enough driftwood to keep them warm and to provide fuel for cooking.

Some members of the family, according to one account, even went in their small boats across the river to St. Boniface Cathedral and tied them up to the cathedral steps while they attended service.

The floods from 1852 to 1948 were relatively smaller than the earlier disasters, but the Red River came up fairly high in 1948 and moved city council to adopt a proposal for spending $1.1 million to create a diking system that was intended to protect the low-lying parts the city from rising waters.

Two years later, the rivers began to rise ominously and, by 19 May 1950, the Red River was more than 40 kilometres (25 mi.) wide. Large areas of Winnipeg were evacuated. Polio victims in their iron lungs were among the fifteen hundred patients taken to other cities for safety.

The armed forces were called in, and thousands of volunteers and hundreds of machines went to work to build dikes—the dikes the city had never gotten around to building under that 1948 plan.

On the farms and in the small towns south of Winnipeg, people either diked their homes or departed, after moving their stock to higher ground. In the city, thousands of homes in Norwood, St. Vital, Fort Garry, and other areas were waterlogged to the second storey. One man paddled into his living room in his canoe.

The cost of rehabilitation was enormous, as was the bill for efforts to stop the water by diking. The net result, about a dozen years later, was the construction of the Winnipeg Floodway and the flood control gates on the Red River at St. Norbert. The floodway, a diversionary channel nearly 47 kilometres (29 mi.) long, stretching from St. Norbert to the Red River south of Selkirk, required more earth to be moved than for the Panama Canal, the Suez Canal, or the St. Lawrence Seaway.

Now, when high water threatens Winnipeg, the floodgates on the river are closed, and a huge volume of water rushes through the new channel, back into the Red River at a place where excess water doesn't threaten life and property.

The biggest scare in the 1997 flood happened when people realized that floodwater was going to rise high enough to enter the city from the west. That prompted the emergency building of a 40-kilometre (25 mi.) dike southwest of Winnipeg known as the Brunkild Dike.

The Floodway has performed so well over the years that, as the twenty-first century began, plans were put in place to significantly widen and deepen it, further protecting lives and property in Winnipeg. The Floodway was constructed by the government of Premier Duff Roblin and was dubbed "Duff's Ditch" by those who doubted that it would work. The term is still commonly used, but now without a hint of derision.

James Dickson
and the Métis
Liberation Army

*This Métis party is similar to the kind that General
Dickson wished to recruit for his "freedom army."*

In most countries and during most ages of history, adventurous fellows with an overdose of ambition and a total disregard for the rules of the game have tried to carve out private empires for themselves. Many of those who succeeded ultimately became respectable, while those who failed suffered a variety of fates—most of them unpleasant.

The United States produced a number of such swashbucklers. Aaron Burr, James Wilkinson, William Walker, Hayden Edwards, and Sam Houston are just a few who planned or actually led expeditions against the Spaniards in the New World and against Mexico and Nicaragua.

There was one freebooter, however, with a close and entertaining link to the Selkirk district, shortly after Lord Selkirk's heirs had sold the settlement back to the Hudson's Bay Company in 1834. The company was responsible for law and order in the whole of its vast domain. It dealt with its responsibilities in the territory, which it had reacquired, by revamping the old Council of Assiniboia, enlarging it, and adding some new members, including Cuthbert Grant, the Métis leader. Grant became a Justice of the Peace for his Grantown district.

In December 1836, a bedraggled and half-starved group of men arrived at Fort Garry, led by one who styled himself "General" James Dickson. He and his party wore the remnants of what had once been ornate, splendid, and expensive uniforms and, on their arrival, they immediately announced the purpose of their journey.

A man of somewhat mysterious origins, Dickson had cut rather a fine figure in both New York and Washington. There, he announced, he was the "liberator of the Indian Nations." He had, he said, lived for some time in Mexico, and at times he referred to himself as "Montezuma II," using the name of the last Aztec ruler.

Dickson seemed to have plenty of money, although the sources of his funding were hazy, and he spent freely in publicizing his aims and in recruiting a corps of "officers" for his freedom army. Everyone in his entourage was outfitted with expensive tailored uniforms, and his was the most flamboyant, thick with gold lace and braid. Somehow he had acquired a sword of the style and workmanship proper for a British general, and with his accoutrements and commanding manner, he cut quite a swath. Bearded and mustachioed, Dickson's handsome face bore marks that might have been saber scars, adding to the air of mystery and glamour that surrounded him.

Dickson's plan, he said, was to go to the Red River Settlement to recruit Métis "cavalry" who, he had heard, were the finest on the continent. He first went to Montreal, where he persuaded some Métis youths, whose fathers were HBC officers, to join him, thinking their presence would help convince their Red River relatives to enlist in his crusade.

Once he had his cavalry—several hundred was the figure mentioned—Dickson planned to march south and west to Santa Fe (then part of Mexico), liberate the Indians, and build for himself and his followers an empire in California, with himself as ruler.

Dickson chartered a ship in Buffalo, New York, and in August 1836 led his sixty followers aboard for the first part of their recruiting trip to the head of Lake Superior. For some unknown reason, the baggage he brought with him included artificial beards and moustaches for his clean-shaven followers—and a suit of chain mail.

As they approached the western end of Lake Huron, however, their ship was wrecked. When they finally arrived at Sault Ste. Marie, they were arrested on the charge that one of the ship's crew had stolen a cow. The enforced halt gave American officials time to investigate the party. They were suspicious because of all of Dickson's talk about his plans.

Finally, they were allowed to leave but, by then, some of the adventurers had become disillusioned and deserted. Dickson's "army," much reduced in size, made its way to the Mississippi River by boat.

While Dickson and his men battled wintry weather on the overland trail from the Mississippi to Red River, the HBC took alarm at the possible invasion of the Red River area. Governor George Simpson was in Detroit on his way east when he learned of Dickson's plans. The Forks, where the Red and Assiniboine Rivers met, was a vital point in the HBC's trade network, and the Métis were necessary to the survival of the colony, since they alone had the skills, numbers, and discipline learned on the buffalo hunt to protect the settlement.

Simpson was also worried about the fact that one of Dickson's chief supporters was a son of Kenneth McKenzie, who continued to challenge the HBC monopoly of the western fur trade.

During the long trek north, by foot and by dogsled, Dickson's party was further diminished as individuals became lost and died of exposure. It was a sorry band of twelve that arrived at Fort Garry shortly before Christmas. Their grandiose expedition had cost them four months and most of their manpower, which was further reduced when HBC officials succeeded in luring away some of the Métis "officers" Dickson had recruited in Montreal by offering them good jobs.

In addition, on Simpson's orders, company officials refused to accept Dickson's bank drafts and, without funds, the rest of his people deserted him. Dickson was trapped at Red River for the winter. However, he had somehow managed to bring quite a large amount of his equipment with him through all the perils he had encountered, and his charismatic personality and resplendent uniforms made him an outstanding and sought-after man in a settlement starved for diversions.

Dickson met Cuthbert Grant, stayed with him for a time, and so effectively used his personal charm and skills that, in the spring of 1837, Grant provided him with the necessary carts, horses, food, and guides to start him off on his long-delayed expedition to Mexico.

It must have been quite a scene as many of the residents of Grantown assembled for the departure. Somewhat threadbare but still splendid, Dickson delivered a speech thanking Grant for his hospitality and help.

Then, doffing his general's hat, he bowed to Grant and, according to the Grant family memoirs, said, "You are the great soldier and leader; I am a failure. These belong to you and not to me." He presented his sword to Grant, whisked off his epaulettes and put them on the shoulders of Grant's coat, jumped on his horse, and rode off into the sunset.

Dickson faded from history. His great adventure was retold in a 1923 booklet entitled *James Dickson: A Filibuster in Minnesota in 1836*, written by Grace Lee Nute and published by the Mississippi Historical Society.

Dickson's epaulettes were placed on the altar of the White Horse Plain Church but were lost when the church burned. The sword was kept in Grant's home for a number of years, but disappeared until it was recovered and identified by historian Margaret Arnett MacLeod, author of a 1963 Grant biography. It was being used on a farm near Grant's former home to cut weeds. It was later identified as an 1810 general's sword of British pattern, the authentication being made by the Tower of London's Master of Arms.

The Wrong Man for the Job

Adam Thom was the first person trained in the law to come to the Red River Valley

There is an avenue in the Transcona area of Winnipeg that bears the name of a man who played a major role in the life of the Red River Settlement for fifteen years. However, for all his importance during the time he lived in the settlement, he is now an almost-forgotten figure.

Adam Thom was the first person trained in the law to come to the Red River Valley. Born in Scotland in 1802, Thom graduated from Aberdeen University, taught school briefly, and then moved to Montreal via London, where he edited the *Montreal Herald* before and during the Rebellion of 1837. His editorial policy and the pamphlets he wrote "denounced the doctrine of French nationality and [did] much to bring on the Rebellion," according to historian E. E. Rich.

In 1838 Lord Durham was named governor of Canada, which then was made up of two provinces, Upper Canada (Ontario) and Lower Canada (Quebec). Among his duties, Durham was instructed to look into the causes of the Rebellion.

Thom took a jaundiced view of Durham and his ideas in the *Herald*, but Durham effectively neutralized the bad press by appointing Thom a commissioner to investigate and report on municipal government in Lower Canada. Thom became one of Durham's secretaries and went back to England with him where he helped to write the report that created a new constitutional set-up in the colony.

The *Durham Report* noted the "deadly animosity that now separates the inhabitants of Lower Canada into the hostile divisions of French and English," and recommended that "it must henceforth be the first purpose of the British Government to establish an English population with English laws and language in this province of Lower Canada, and to trust its government to none but a decidedly English legislature." As Roy Stubbs remarks in his book, *Four Recorders of Rupert's Land*, "If these words were Durham's own, the sentiment they expressed was certainly Thom's."

After finishing his work with Durham, Thom accepted the Hudson's Bay Company's offer of the newly created position of recorder of Rupert's Land. The recorder was not a judge, though he sat as senior member of the Court of General Sessions in the territory and, in addition, was responsible for administrative matters in connection with enforcement of the law. He was backed by the authority of the HBC, his employer, and always upheld the view that all law in Rupert's Land sprang from the original charter given to the Company by King Charles II. In fact, subsequent legal opinions have held that the law in Rupert's Land was that which was in force in England at the time the charter was granted.

There was a limit on the recorder's authority. He could only hold a preliminary hearing in cases where a death penalty might be imposed. Under these circumstances, if evidence warranted, he was instructed to ship the accused and witnesses to face trial in Upper Canada. He was required to assemble a jury in all criminal cases and in all civil cases involving sums of between ten and two hundred pounds; the latter amount was the highest on which he could render judgment.

Thom took a wide view of his mandate, and his opinions and decisions were reinforced by his appearance and manner. He was tall, heavily built, strong-featured, and ponderous in his speech, which never lost the strong Aberdeen accent of his youth. Thick-browed, stern-eyed, and totally convinced of his mission, he must have been a somewhat daunting presence to the many who appeared before him.

In spite of the restrictions on his authority, soon after his arrival Thom presided over a case in which a Saulteaux was tried and hanged for the murder of two other Natives, one a Sioux and the other a Saulteaux. The entire matter—murder, arrest, trial, and execution—was resolved within four days.

Some twelve years later, in 1857, a Select Committee of the British House of Commons investigated this event and was told by a witness that there was confusion over the identity of the accused; that, although a jury was present, the accused had no one to assist in his defence; that the valley residents were aware that the local court could not pass a sentence of death; and that there was no protest against the summary execution because all the colonists were "too much under the control of the [Hudson's Bay] Company; the Company would stop the supplies."

Roy St. George Stubbs expresses the view that this first execution in the west might well have been a "wanton miscarriage of justice."

While in office, Thom codified and clarified a number of local laws that had been passed by the Council of Assiniboia. There was no doubt that he filled a long-needed position in the community and was in many ways deserving of the description written in 1890 by Archer Martin in the *Western Law Times*: "The father of the bench and bar in Western Canada."

Thom was involved in the celebrated Sayer trial in which Guillaume Sayer, with three others, was charged with breaching the HBC monopoly through illegal fur trading. The presence of several hundred armed Métis in and around the courthouse was enough to cause the court to withhold sentencing, although it had found Sayer guilty. This inaction fatally weakened the HBC's efforts to enforce its trade policy.

In 1849, following the Sayer trial, the Canadian and Métis residents of the Red River Valley made several demands, the first of which was to call for "the immediate removal of Mr. Recorder Thom from the Settlement."

With the Sayer trial went any goodwill Thom had developed with the non-English part of the population. Then, he lost much of his credibility among the English because of his role in the Ballenden defamation trial of 1850 when, as one of the defendants pointed out, Thom sat as a magistrate in a case in which he had been legal counsel for the plaintiff.

As a result of the furor his actions had aroused, Thom was demoted from recorder to clerk of the court, though he had the same pay of seven hundred pounds a year. Even then, he was unable to appear in court because of the hostility of the Métis.

Adam Thom left Red River in 1854, sailing for Britain from York Factory with his wife and son, Adam, on the HBC ship *Prince of Wales*. After short stays in Edinburgh and Torquay, he settled in London. His wife predeceased him, and he died in 1890. His son subsequently came back to Canada and settled in Galt, Ontario.

Almost everyone who left written accounts of life in the mid–1800s in Red River had something to say about Adam Thom.

Alexander Ross wrote in *The Red River Settlement, its Rise, Progress and Present State* (1856): "He may be said to have always had his own way . . . and this often raised up difficulties between himself and his colleagues . . . He possessed the gift of twisting and untwisting his interpretations so as always to fit his own cause."

J. J. Hargrave wrote in *Red River* (1871): "At the close of his long and often unquiet sojourn, he left behind the reputation of great ability and of kindly hospitality."

D. Gunn and C. R. Tuttle wrote in *History of Manitoba* (1880): "As Recorder, no objection was raised, but as Judge to deal with cases, many of which were between the settlers and the Company, it was felt that justice was more likely to be obtained from someone who was not a paid servant of the Company."

There may be some grounds for questioning Thom's legal ability. While still editor of the *Montreal Herald*, he was articled to a Montreal law firm for the purpose of obtaining his qualifications. Because of his degree from Aberdeen University, he was called to the Quebec Bar after only one year of articling. Although his Scottish shrewdness and sublime faith in his own rightness may have enabled him to put that one year of training to practical use, the fact remains that he had only a superficial knowledge of the law and his prejudice coloured many of his judgments.

The Young and the Restless on the Frontier

Fort Garry, at the forks of the Red and Assiniboine Rivers, was the site of many a real-life drama.

MANITOBA ARCHIVES (FORT GARRY 5)

A century before the advent of the soap opera, the Red River Valley experienced its own real-life drama, not far removed from the fantastic stories told on daytime television today.

In December 1836 John Ballenden, a respected young clerk for the Hudson's Bay Company, took eighteen-year-old Sarah McLeod as his wife. Sarah was the daughter of Chief Trader Archibald R. McLeod and his Native wife. She was described as "a delightful creature" by historian James Hargrave, who added that John Ballenden "had every reason to consider himself a happy man."

The Ballendens lived at various HBC posts until 1848, when John was promoted and made responsible for the company's affairs in the Red River area. Their move to Red River placed Sarah at the peak of the social order in a community that was gradually growing as more fur trade families chose it for retirement. It also made it possible for the Ballendens' two daughters to attend the Red River Academy.

Sarah arranged a number of dinners and parties and sometimes presided at the officers' mess in Upper Fort Garry at the forks of the Red and Assiniboine Rivers. From 1846 to 1848, the fort had been the headquarters for 350 soldiers of the Royal Regiment of Foot (RRF). When the RRF went back to England, military duties were taken over by a force of less than one hundred officers and men from various British regiments. Known as the Chelsea Pensioners, they were commanded by Major W. B. Caldwell, who was also governor of the Red River area, which was then known as the District of Assiniboia.

At the same time as Sarah was taking a prominent role in the settlement, a number of English and Scottish women—wives of company officials and missionaries—arrived in the district. It seems they had not been well informed about life in fur-trade country, and were more than a little irked to find that a woman of mixed race was, as a note in the HBC Archives says, "destined to raise her whole caste above European ladies in their influence on society here." The feelings of the European women about Sarah's status were not openly expressed at first, but two arrivals in 1849 changed all that.

Anne Clouston arrived from Britain as the fiancée of HBC clerk A. E. Pelly. Anne's father was the HBC agent at Stromness in the Shetland Islands, and the groom-to-be was related to Sir John Pelly, HBC governor in London. On the same ship came Margaret Anderson, sister of the Right Reverend David Anderson, the first Anglican bishop of Rupert's Land. The bishop married Clouston and Pelly at York Factory, after which the newlyweds, the bishop, and his sister made the long boat trip south to Red River.

Bishop Anderson was a widower with three small children. He had persuaded his sister to come out to take charge of his household and to help run the struggling Red River Academy for young ladies. Margaret Anderson was described by a contemporary as "a straitlaced, sharp-tongued spinster." Both Margaret and the new Mrs. Pelly soon found the local social situation not to their liking.

Letitia Hargrave, whose letters from Red River provide a considerable insight into life in the little community, was astounded at Anne's pretensions, to say nothing of the size and variety of her trousseau, which was as large "as if she had been going to Calcutta."

Anne was given, according to Sylvia Van Kirk, to "fastidious and fainting ways," which produced amused comments and reactions from many of those who lived in or near the upper fort, especially from "[Captain Christopher] Foss who evidently was in the habit of casting mocking glances at Mrs. Ballenden," whenever Anne's behaviour became too extreme.

In fact, the situation reached a point where Anne "made herself ill." A. E. Pelly thereupon refused to dine in the officers' mess at the fort and would have nothing to do with the Ballendens. This must have resulted in some serious problems, since Pelly was a junior on John Ballenden's staff.

It was not long before a distinct clique developed with Anne Pelly at its centre. This group set about casting aspersions on Sarah Ballenden, among them rumours that Captain Foss's friendship with Sarah was a sign of a more intimate relationship.

Hargrave's letters quote Mrs. Robert Logan as saying that Sarah was one of those women who "must always have a sweetheart as well as a husband" and also noted the current opinion that Foss's attentions to Sarah were "of such a character as to entitle Mr. B[allenden] to a divorce."

Anne Pelly, it seems, relayed all this gossip to Major Caldwell, demanding that he do something to show that such behaviour could not be accepted. Caldwell was in an unenviable position. He could not side with Anne and her colleagues without alienating John Ballenden, who had considerable influence as the chief HBC officer of the district. But he could not brush aside the complaints and gossip of the European women. His chance to address the issue came when John Ballenden left in June 1849 for a meeting out west with George Simpson, governor of Rupert's Land.

Caldwell immediately seized the opportunity and ordered his family to have nothing to do with the Ballendens. The bishop and his sister snubbed Sarah Ballenden and her daughters, and Anglican missionary Reverend William Cockran passed the word to some of Sarah's nearest friends that she was unfit for their company.

In such a small and closely knit society as the Red River Settlement, the rumours spread quickly and people began to take sides. Sarah's reputation was defended by a number of highly placed people, including Dr. John Bunn (who was himself of mixed ancestry) and recorder, Adam Thom. Thom's opinions of Natives, the French of Quebec, and the mixed-race members of the Red River district were not, to put it mildly, very high. Still, Thom supported Sarah, despite her Native ancestry.

As a result of the word-of-mouth allegations about Sarah and Foss, tension in the district grew. Finally, Foss brought a defamation suit against A. E. Pelly and his wife Anne, HBC clerk John Black and his wife, and a third person who was a minor character in the matter, on Sarah's and his own behalf.

The case was heard by Thom in his capacity as magistrate. There were at the time, and have been since, numerous questions raised about his fitness to hear and judge on the charges, since he had openly advised Sarah before the lawsuit was started. However, he was the only person in the district with the authority to try the case.

The court sat for three days and numerous witnesses were called for both sides. According to all the written accounts, there was little evidence given under oath that could not be described as rumour or hearsay. The sessions drew a large number of spectators, and, outside the courtroom, arguments raged and tempers became heated.

Finally, Thom announced his verdict: Sarah and Foss had indeed been the victims of a slander campaign that had injured their reputations and their standing in the community. The Pellys were ordered to pay five hundred pounds sterling (a very large amount then), and the Blacks, one hundred pounds.

Meanwhile, Caldwell had been replaced as governor of Assiniboia by Eden Colville, who was sent out by HBC headquarters in London to calm some of the disagreements, which were not only disrupting the community, but were also thought to be harmful to the efficient and profitable operation of the company.

Colville reported regularly in long and detailed letters to the company in London. In some of these, he had high praise for John Ballenden for his excellent work on behalf of the HBC and marked him for future promotion, although he had some reservations about Ballenden's health.

Writing about clerk John Black and A. E. Pelly, he was less than kind, describing Black as being of little worth unless closely supervised. He also had some rather pointed things to say about Captain Foss, noting his tendency to gamble and the debts he had run up while at Red River.

Such gambling activities conducted by Foss include one win, however, that might have encouraged John Black in his efforts to defame Foss and Sarah Ballenden. In fact, one of those who left records of the time neatly provided Black's motives when she/he wrote that Foss had won a considerable sum of money from Black; that before Foss' arrival, Black had made more-than-friendly advances to Sarah and had been sent packing; and that Black was envious of Ballenden's position in the company and had ambitions to replace him.

In a letter written in August 1850, Colville reported to Sir John Pelly that Mrs. Ballenden had at last been shown in her true colours. He described a letter to Captain Foss, purportedly written by Sarah, which started off, "My darling Christopher."

Colville described how Foss was ostracized by almost everyone in the settlement, except the family at whose home he was living. He also claimed to have knowledge of a visit Sarah had paid to Foss' lodgings and added that Bunn and Thom appeared to have withdrawn their support for Sarah.

John Ballenden was away on company business and, during his absence, his wife was forced by the growing atmosphere of hostility to seek refuge with a family at St. Andrews. She then moved to Norway House.

According to Sylvia Van Kirk, John Ballenden obtained leave and returned to his native Scotland, taking Sarah with him. Sarah died of tuberculosis in Edinburgh in 1853. Her husband returned to his post at the upper fort and was there to welcome his two daughters, Annie and Elizabeth, on their return from school in England.

The two daughters lived on at Red River for the rest of their lives. The older daughter, Elizabeth, married William Bannatyne, a member of a wealthy pioneer merchant family, and lived for many years at Sturgeon Creek. Annie Ballenden became the wife of William McMurray, who was for a time in charge of the HBC post at Pembina. She died at an early age.

Captain Foss eventually went back to England, but under what circumstances and to what future no record is easily available.

The Sisters of Charity

A Sister of Charity (Grey Nun) visits with a Métis family.

MANITOBA ARCHIVES (N10201)

In 1850 a small group of people left Montreal on the long and difficult journey to a tiny isolated settlement on the prairies. Included in the party were three Sisters of Charity, part of the Order of Grey Nuns, and two novices. Their destination was the mission at St. Boniface, across the Red River from the Hudson's Bay Company post at Fort Garry and the struggling settlement started thirty-eight years earlier by Lord Selkirk.

One of these devoted travellers was Sister Laurent who later, at the age of ninety-two, was interviewed about her experiences by W. J. Healy. Healy was Manitoba's provincial librarian and he published Sister Laurent's story in his 1923 book *Women of Red River* (see sidebar, "Women of Red River").

Sister Laurent outlived all those who had come west with her, and Healy found her to be a treasury of recollections of those long-past days. She described how she had come from a home on St. Antoine Street in Montreal, where her father was a leather worker, and how her whole family was devoted to the Roman Catholic faith. Sister Laurent took her final vows in the Order of the Sisters of Charity when she was eighteen. Almost immediately, she volunteered to go to the west in response to an appeal from Bishop J. N. Provencher, who had been in the Red River district since 1818 and had been appointed bishop in 1822.

On his way east, Bishop Provencher had asked members of the Grey Nuns order in American cities for volunteers to serve in the west, but was unable to obtain any help from them. He was more successful in Montreal, and as a result Sister Laurent, Sister Fiset, and Sister L'Esperance joined the religious establishment in St. Boniface.

The 1850 arrivals were not the first Grey Nuns in the Red River region. Sisters Valade, Lagrave, Coutlee, and LaFrance had made the journey six years earlier and had started almost immediately to teach school and carry out other work done by the order. The Grey Nuns had an indirect connection with Red River—the order had been founded in 1737 by Marie Marguerite d'Youville, a relative of Pierre La Verendrye, the first European to reach the Red River Valley in his

Women of Red River

This region has always had its share of historical writers—Alexander Begg, George Bryce, and Mary Fitzgibbon to name a few—but Manitoba provincial librarian W. J. Healy's 1923 book, Women of Red River, was the first to concentrate on the lives of women in the tiny isolated settlement around the forks of the Red and Assiniboine Rivers.

By the time Healy started to gather his material, the women who had come to the Red River Settlement in the first groups of settlers—from 1812 to 1815— were long dead, but many of their direct descendents still lived in Manitoba and many of them carried memories of stories their parents and grandparents had told them.

Healy begins with a chapter about the first white women in the west. The first, he writes, was a nameless young Scottish woman who disguised herself as a man and followed her sweetheart to Red River. On 29 December 1807, she bore a child whom she took back to Scotland with her when she returned there the following summer.

The first European child born in Manitoba is thus unidentified, but not so the second, who was born on 6 January 1808, the daughter of Jean and Marie Anne Lagimodière. This child would become the mother of Louis Riel, the controversial and charismatic Métis leader.

The next women to arrive here were the eighteen who accompanied the second group of Selkirk settlers in 1812. Another twenty women arrived in the spring of 1813 after a winter at Churchill and a hundred-mile trip on foot to York Factory where they boarded York boats for the long upriver voyage to where Winnipeg now stands.

In spite of its isolation, Healy writes, the women interviewed remembered the Red River Settlement has having a "peaceful, pastoral community life." Storms, drought, hail, and grasshoppers plagued the settlers, and their misfortunes culminated in the great flood of 1826, when the only safe ground was at Stony Mountain, or Bird's Hill.

One of the oldest women whose memories Healy recorded was Mrs. William Cowan, born to the Sinclair family in 1832 on the east bank of the Red River, just north of present-day Winnipeg. Her grandfather, James Curtis Bird, owned 1,214 hectares (300 acres) running east from the Red River to Bird's Hill. In her ninety-first year, Mrs. Cowan retold the stories she had heard from eyewitnesses of the ride of the Métis, led by Cuthbert Grant, on their way to the fateful Battle of Seven Oaks.

There is little, if any, unkindness in Healy's words, even if the reader catches undercurrents of disapproval from some of the men whose names are indelibly matched to Winnipeg's heritage. And the women vividly convey humour, pathos, happiness, and tragedy, though softened by the passage of the years, their feelings about their history as real as they once were when they experienced those far-off times.

explorations and fur trading expeditions.

In 1850 the long trip from Montreal was made by boats and canoes on river and lake, and by stagecoach until they reached St. Paul, from which they started out across the open prairies north to Red River.

"I was happy all the time," Sister Laurent remembered. "We did not like the pemmican at first as we came over the plains. When we saw the Indians I said to Sister L'Esperance, 'At least we are among the red men of the plains of whom we have read.'"

Sister Laurent remembered how a member of the first group of Grey Nuns to arrive there, Sister Lagrave, worked hard to beautify the interior of the first cathedral. "It was Sister Lagrave who sat upon a chair on a board away up high and painted the walls," she said. "Sometimes she would have two or three of the sisters away up there helping her, but most of them trembled when they saw her go up so high." Sister Lagrave was also credited with carving a statue of the Virgin and making the crib and figure of the infant Jesus for the Christmas tableau.

Sister Laurent and her companions brought with them documents appointing Father Alexandre A. Taché as bishop coadjutor to Bishop Provencher. After delivering the documents, they were allowed a few days to rest and accustom themselves to their new home. But they were soon deeply involved in the work of the order, which included regular visits to all of the homes in the area.

After Sister Laurent had been in St. Boniface for a short time, she was asked to teach in the school the order had established for the settlers' children. "When I opened the door and saw those big boys, I had doubts, and I said, 'I do not want to teach school. Those boys are too big, and they will not mind me, I am sure,'" Healy recorded.

Instead, Sister Laurent was given the duty of visiting homes in the district to help in any way she could. "At first," she told Healy, "they gave me a horse and rig, but I used to have to get out and tie the horse at each house, and then untie him and get in again, so I told them I would rather use my own two feet."

The first autumn after they arrived, all the sisters in the mission went out into the fields to help with the harvest in the farm plots next to the convent. Sister Laurent told Healy that she remembered this quite well, and that she had also volunteered to help: "But after I had used the sickle a little while they would not let me do any more with it. They said I slashed with it too quickly, and they were afraid I would cut myself."

Sisters who visited homes in the community were expected to do any task that needed to be done. One of the most important was nursing, and, although all took a hand in this, the order tended to assign specific work to those who were best at it.

Among the diseases they encountered and were expected to treat to the best of their abilities were dysentery, measles, smallpox, and inflammatory rheumatism. "We had medicines we had brought from Montreal," Sister Laurent told Healy, "but we also learned the use of herbs that grew in the country."

Within eight years of their arrival, Sisters Laurent and Desautels had founded another convent at St. Norbert; a third had been set up on the White Horse Plain west of Fort Garry. Later, Sister Laurent became the sister superior of the St. Norbert convent and, still later, housekeeper at the St. Boniface establishment.

Sister Laurent immersed herself so deeply in her work that she had little time or occasion to think of visiting her Montreal home. However, after five years in the west, she was offered a chance to go to Montreal with the group making the annual trip for supplies. Then, shortly before the departure day, one of the other sisters received word from Montreal that her mother was gravely ill, so Sister Laurent gave up her place. She never did return east; she felt that her responsibilities and her love of the work she was doing were more important.

"When I came here," she said at age ninety-two, "I came to stay. And now that I can no longer work, I pray for them. It comes to you that you cannot be happy living for yourself. You want to help the little children, the poor people, and the old ones. It is not leaving the world—it is just doing something you want to do."

The Last Great Battle of the Plains

A band of Sioux on the march in 1874.

It has been more than 150 years since the buffalo hunters of Red River met their traditional enemies, the Sioux, in the last great battle of the plains—the Battle of the Grand Coteau.

The bold, energetic, and warlike Sioux occupied the area from the Missouri River north to the southernmost edge of the lands long occupied by the Saulteaux and Cree. For generations, the two groups had fought and raided each other, and the struggle was intensified by the rise of the Métis nation, which made a highly organized expedition of the buffalo hunt.

Like the Métis, the Sioux depended on the buffalo for much of their food, clothing, and other needs. When the twice-yearly hunt, carried on like a military operation by the Métis, drove the big herds of bison farther west and south, the Sioux felt the pinch severely. For many years prior to the last big battle in 1851, small parties from each side had attacked each other, with a gradually rising toll of casualties.

In June 1851 the St. Boniface–St. Norbert Métis hunting party, accompanied by Reverend Albert Lacombe, went south to meet the Pembina hunt and then turned west for their rendezvous with the hunters from St. Francois Xavier, led by Cuthbert Grant's nephew, Jean Baptiste Falcon. The Métis of St. Boniface and Pembina were no longer willing to accept the leadership of Grant, who had lost much prestige as a result of his attitude during the Sayer trial two years before.

The St. Boniface–St. Norbert group included thirteen hundred people, 318 of them hunters. The St. Francois party was much smaller, consisting of only sixty-seven hunters and possibly twice that number of women and children. It was accompanied by missionary Father Louis Lafleche.

After hunting near each other for several days, the two groups became separated by several miles. On 12 July, the St. Francois scouts encountered a large encampment of Sioux, variously estimated to number from fifteen to twenty-five hundred. Five of the scouts who went too close were captured by the Sioux, but two managed to break away and rode to warn their colleagues.

Falcon immediately prepared for an attack. The wagons were circled with their livestock in the centre. Women and children occupied trenches dug under the carts, while the seventy-seven men and boys able to handle guns made rifle pits outside the wagon circle. They did not know what the odds were, Lafleche later said, but were not very hopeful of being able to withstand an attack by such large numbers of warriors.

Falcon sent two messengers to carry the news to the larger Métis hunting party and, on Sunday, 13 July, after Father Lafleche said Mass and heard confessions, they took their places and awaited the onslaught.

Hundreds of Sioux appeared on the crest of a nearby ridge, where they paused. A small group of Métis rode out to warn the Indians that they should leave the hunters alone and to offer them some presents. The Sioux ignored the gifts and demanded everything in the camp.

Meanwhile, one of the Métis held by the Sioux—named McGillis—suddenly broke free and galloped madly to reach his colleagues, warning them there were two thousand Sioux about to attack.

The Sioux then charged, trying to break up the wagon circle. They were led by a young man who, Falcon later said, "was so beautiful that my heart revolted at the necessity of killing him." Beautiful or not, the young Sioux was killed in the initial attack. Lafleche, meanwhile, had put on his white surplice and, crucifix in hand, went around the carts, helping soothe the children as he encouraged the adults. Later, he remarked that he had not carried a gun, but did have a hatchet ready so that he could fight to the end beside the Métis if the circle was broken.

The first charge was beaten off and, as the Sioux paused to regroup, the two remaining Métis prisoners—Whiteford and Malaterre—made a dash for freedom. With the better horse, Whiteford made it, but Malaterre was killed and his body dismembered to terrify the Métis.

The next day the Sioux surrounded the camp, making short rushes and sniping attacks, with young warriors every now and then charging the circle in a wild effort to get through. But the circle held, and after awhile the Sioux withdrew. They were unwilling to accept the heavy casualties they had suffered. However, as they looked at the relatively small numbers of the Métis and counted their own losses, their anger grew and they made a second wild attack.

This fared no better than the first. Although they kept up harassing tactics for about six hours, they were obviously crestfallen over their failure to conquer quickly. Some blamed their failure on Father Lafleche's presence, saying, "The French have a Manitou with them. We shall never come to the end of them. It is impossible to kill them."

The Sioux began to remove their wounded on the carts they had brought to haul away the loot they had expected to win, and a violent thunderstorm added to their discomfort. In addition, the Sioux scouts watching the main hunting party brought word that a large number of armed hunters was rapidly approaching the battle scene.

On 14 July, the Sioux did not attack, and Falcon and his colleagues decided to make a daring and dangerous attempt to join the main hunting party. The wagon train was organized so that it could be quickly transformed into a defensive circle, and mounted patrols covered all the avenues of approach. They moved out but, after an hour, their scouts warned that another attack was coming. Quickly, the circle was reformed, new rifle pits dug, and stock corralled.

For five hours the party endured a series of charges and sniping attacks, but the circle remained firm and a thunderstorm that came growling up over the ridges of the Grand Coteau brought an end to the fight.

A Sioux chief, hand raised in the sign of peace, asked permission to enter the camp. On being told to go away, he replied that his people had had enough and would never again attack the Métis hunters. However, in a final gesture of defiance, the Sioux raced past the camp at a gallop, waving lances and guns, and firing a last volley of musket balls and arrows. The rain started as they disappeared over the ridge.

To their surprise, the Métis found that only three men had been wounded in that final storm of shot, and as they gave thanks for their deliverance, a large body of men from the main hunting party arrived. The Sioux dead numbered eighty, with many more wounded and the loss of many horses.

The Battle of the Grand Coteau established Métis control of the plains, and confirmed both their basic tactics and their daring in moving across open ground in the proximity of an enemy force of vastly superior numbers.

A Positive View
of Negatives

Himes photograph of the Saskatchewan Exploring
Expedition camped on the Red River, 1 June 1858

Snap! Click! And in a few seconds you can have your finished pictures. Even if your camera is not a Polaroid, picture taking is now a snap. Everything is automatic, with film available everywhere and one-hour photo services welcoming your business. With the advent of digital cameras, you can even print your own photographs without leaving your house.

It wasn't always this way, of course. Today's camera-laden tourist has it easy compared to the toils and troubles endured by the first photographer ever to capture the Manitoba scene in emulsion.

The Canadian pioneer of the lens and shutter was Humphrey Lloyd Hime, who came here to ply his trade, albeit in a scientific sense, more than 140 years ago, when he arrived at Fort Garry as part of the Canadian exploration party sent out to report on the western country.

In the mid-nineteenth century, Canada consisted simply of Upper and Lower Canada, now Ontario and Quebec. Confederation was only a dream, and "from sea to sea" little more than a twinkle in the eyes of a few visionaries. Canadians were concerned about two things in those days. One was the approaching date for renewal, or termination, of the Hudson's Bay Company's charter to rule a quarter of the continent. The other was the certain knowledge that many people in the United States were casting their eyes northward. Americans were referring to what they called "Manifest Destiny," a sort of heaven-bestowed mandate to the American people to go out and fill up the empty spaces of the new world. So both the British government—because it controlled the HBC's future—and the Canadian government sent expeditions to report on the geography, climate, soil, water, natural resources, and people of these empty and windswept plains.

The British expedition was led by Captain John Palliser, whose name has been immortalized in the Palliser Triangle label stuck on a semi-arid area of the west. The leader of the Canadian expedition was George Gladman. This expedition was divided into three groups, with one of them under the command of Henry Youle Hind, a professor of geology and natural history at Trinity College, Toronto. After returning from a preliminary survey in 1857, Hind again set out for the west and took with him Humphrey Lloyd Hime, listed on the expedition's payroll as a photographer with additional surveying duties.

Hime, born in Ireland but having lived in Canada since 1854, was a junior partner in the survey and photography firm of Armstrong, Beere, and Hime. Hind offered him the position on the Canadian expedition and recommended him most highly when he asked the government to approve his appointment.

Hind's exploration party went by train to Detroit where it boarded a steamer for the trip to Grand Portage on Lake Superior, a few miles south of present-day Thunder Bay. Hind intended to make the journey to the Red River Settlement, which was to be his headquarters, by following the old North West Company canoe route via Pigeon River, Rainy River, Lake of the Woods, and Winnipeg River.

In preparing for his trip, Hime had much more to do than pack a camera bag and another satchel full of film. He required plain-glass plates, a vast array of chemicals for preparing the plates to receive photographic impressions, and another massive quantity of chemicals to develop the pictures. In addition, he needed a lightproof tent in which to prepare his plates for exposure and to do his processing after the pictures were taken. The whole outfit cost in the neighbourhood of $250, a tidy sum in those days. It was an outlay from which the government and Hind expected great things.

The numerous portages on the chosen route meant that Hime's equipment, along with all the other paraphernalia of the expedition, had to be carried several times between rivers and lakes. His tent for photography weighed nearly 6 kilograms (13 lb.), and his other materials must have run from about 32 to 36 kilograms (70 to 80 lb.).

Hime's first, and only moderately successful attempt at photography in the field was at Fort Frances, where the party rested for a day. No other pictures were taken until they reached the mouth of the Red River, where Hime took a photograph of the party as they relaxed in front of their canoes.

After a few days at Upper Fort Garry, they set off westward, with five Red River carts, a wagon, two canoes, and all their equipment and instruments. They stopped briefly at St. James Church (opposite Polo Park) and then went west to Prairie Portage (now Portage la Prairie), up the Souris River, along the international boundary, then north, aiming for Fort Ellice at the junction of the Qu'Appelle and Assiniboine Rivers. There, Hime had the chance to take one picture, which Hind later praised highly.

At the junction, the expedition broke up into three parties to explore different areas. Hime's job was to travel to Last Mountain Lake and then on to Fort Pelly to join the others.

Hime's account of this journey includes a description of a near tragedy at the crossing of the White Sand River. The very steep banks made it necessary to "stage up the carts with another rope before and men on either side to haul . . . the cart upset in the rapids and I had the satisfaction of seeing my Photographic apparatus, my gun, my clothes submerged. Fortunately they were tied tight and did not get out of the cart." Only one photograph, taken at Lake Qu'Appelle, was stained by water. Hime's party later returned to Fort Garry by way of the Shell River, Riding Mountain, White Mud River, Prairie Portage, and the trail along the Assiniboine River.

About fifty of Hime's pictures have survived. On the expedition's return to Toronto, prints were made and appended to the expedition's report and were also reproduced in the *Illustrated London News* in England.

Hime went on to a distinguished career as a securities dealer, financial expert, Toronto alderman, Justice of the Peace, and officer and director of a number of companies—but not as a photographer. In fact, there is no evidence that he ever took any more pictures after his arduous expedition to western Canada.

The Graveyard of Daily Papers

Delivering the Winnipeg Tribune to Brandon by
Avro 548 on 28 July 1921.

MANITOBA ARCHIVES (N2495)

In 1856 the American publication *Harper's New Monthly Magazine* wrote of the Red River Settlement: "Deserts almost trackless divide it on all sides from the habitations of civilized man ... Receiving no impressions from without, it reflects none. It sends forth neither newspapers nor books nor correspondents' letters; no paragraph in any newspaper records its weal or woe." The thirty years after that was printed certainly made a difference!

The first newspaper published in what is now Manitoba was the creation of two Ontario printers, William Buckingham and William Coldwell. The first edition of the newspaper called the *Nor'-Wester* came out in December 1859. The *Nor'-Wester* chronicled the events of the Red River Valley settlements until it was suppressed in 1869 by Louis Riel's provisional government. Although ownership of and responsibility for it changed several times during that decade, the *Nor'-Wester* was published weekly with only a couple of brief suspensions in 1860 and 1865.

Coldwell then attempted to produce another weekly paper, the *Red River Pioneer*, but this was banned because it supported the stillborn administration of Governor William McDougall. Riel's government bought Coldwell's Manitoba plant for £550 and started publication of the *New Nation*, printed weekly in English and French. First appearing in January 1870, it was edited for four months by Major N. M. Robinson, an American citizen who was an ardent supporter of American annexation of the Canadian North-West. He was replaced by Thomas Spence.

After this came a stream of weeklies, including a weekly *Free Press*, until 6 July 1874, when the daily *Free Press*, an afternoon newspaper, made its appearance. The *Free Press* has continued publication with several name changes and switches in ownership until the present day. It was founded by W. F. Luxton, who was defeated by Francis Cornish in Winnipeg's first mayoral election. Luxton became ambitious, however, and in selling shares to buy other papers, he lost control of the *Free Press* in 1893. In 1898 the Sifton family acquired the paper.

In those days newspapers, whether weekly or daily, were politically oriented to a degree modern readers would find hard to accept. The federal election of 1872 was so bitterly fought that it is remembered for a series of riots during which every newspaper publishing plant in Winnipeg was attacked and partially or totally destroyed.

The *Free Press* was quickly followed by other dailies—a revived *Nor'-Wester*, a *Manitoba Herald*, a *Daily Times*, a *Daily Tribune, Sun, Call, News Telegram*, another *Nor'-Wester*—most of which appeared on the scene for varying lifespans and then disappeared. Life was hard in the newspaper business then, with larger and stronger papers practicing a kind of cannibalism as they gobbled up the smaller ones.

Winnipeg was not the only place boasting daily papers, predominantly the *Winnipeg Free Press* and the *Winnipeg Tribune*. In the midst of the great land boom in Emerson, that town briefly supported two dailies and three weeklies in 1882, and in 1883, Brandon also had two dailies and three weeklies. Scores of weekly papers were started in the decades that ended the nineteenth century and began the twentieth.

In 1900 newspaper publisher J. H. Galbraith wrote that "by reason of politics there are about twice as many newspapers being published in Manitoba as there is a decent living for . . . a score or more commenced publication, not on business principles but on political principles."

Political papers did not last long, nor did rival journals in small towns. Personality also played a role in the demise of journals and papers as in the case of the *Gladstone Age* and *Westbourne County Farmer*, which folded in 1890 after a run of just over two years. It failed, according to historians, because of the outstanding ability of its editor, Peter Moody, to antagonize almost everyone with whom he came in contact.

Most of Manitoba's newspapers bore fairly traditional names—*Banner, News, Press, Times, Herald*—but some were named outside the normal current of fashion. One such paper was a weekly started in the late 1880s as an antidote to the political one-sidedness and heavy-handed style of the *Gladstone Age*. Named the *Bug* by its founder, J. D. McLaren, it spent its two years of existence poking fun at and lampooning its older rival. About the same time, Hamiota was served by the *Hustler*, which meant a go-getter or entrepreneur, but even then the term was considered to be in poor taste by some. A former Cleveland resident, who came to Souris in 1902, borrowed the name of the *Cleveland Plaindealer* when he started the *Souris Plaindealer*.

The peak period for weeklies in Manitoba was 1910 when there were eighty-seven papers in business. But the luxury of competition in

The Winnipeg Press Club

In the fall of 1988, the Winnipeg Press Club celebrated its one hundredth anniversary. Some newspaper people felt that such an occasion should be marked by more than a dinner and speeches.

A group of from twelve to twenty women and men met in the spring of 1986 to consider a project for the club's centennial. They revived a name traditional in both the publishing and the fur trading business by calling themselves the Nor'Westers and set a goal of trying to gather enough material to produce a history of journalism in Manitoba.

Many former newspaper people who worked in Manitoba and were now scattered across the country were asked to contribute their notes, comments, recollections, or favourite stories.

Many of the modern-day Nor'-Westers had years of experience in the business and knew first-hand most of the outstanding events and unforgettable characters with which Manitoba's politics and journalism have abounded—and still do, to a lamentably lesser degree.

In keeping with the tradition of their craft, the Nor'Westers met their deadline and Torch on the Prairies: A Portrait of Journalism in Manitoba 1859 to 1988 was published in time for the club's centennial.

the press was short-lived. Editors and publishers, who had in many cases set up business with more enthusiasm than capital or local support, found the time of reckoning was at hand.

As a result the decade from 1910 to 1920 saw many changes in the newspaper field. Some publishers simply stopped publication. Others managed to negotiate mergers with their competitors or sold out to someone with a fresh supply of money and optimism.

In addition, since large groups of settlers from various backgrounds had come to Manitoba, the number of ethnic presses grew until all the major languages of Europe were represented. In fact, from 1877 to 1978, there is a record of 161 ethnic papers having been started in Winnipeg alone. By the mid-1980s, there were still sixteen papers produced in Manitoba in languages other than English and French, but by the end of the century this number had dropped considerably.

Winnipeg has been known as the Graveyard of Daily Papers. From the time of the appearance of the *Free Press*'s first daily rival to the present, the city has only twice been a one-newspaper town. On both of those occasions ambitious entrepreneurs have come forward to restore the spice of competition to the newspaper business.

John Schultz,
Scoundrel or Hero?

All that remained in 1913 of the store of John Schultz.

MANITOBA ARCHIVES (WINNIPEG BUILDINGS – BUSINESS – SCHULTZ J.C. 1)

"Tall, powerfully built, intelligent and well-travelled . . . [he] seemed bent on coming into conflict with those of the native-born population of the Settlement whose mother tongue was French."—D. W. Thomson, *Men and Meridians*

"Fate had manufactured a scoundrel out of material meant by Nature for a gentleman."—Unnamed contemporary, quoted in *Manitoba: A History*, by W. L. Morton

"Manitoba never possessed a better friend, Canada a more devoted son, nor the Empire a more loyal subject . . ."—*Winnipeg Free Press*, 1896

These quotes describe not three men, but one—John Christian Schultz. The man who became the stormy petrel of Manitoba politics was born on 1 January 1840 at Amherstburg, Upper Canada. At that time Upper and Lower Canada were linked by one parliament in which each province had equal representation. Representatives of Upper Canada wanted to expand their province, introduce representation by population, and thus give the English-speaking people supremacy over the French-speaking population of Lower Canada.

In the late 1850s, when Schultz was believed to be studying medicine at Queen's University and Victoria (Cobourg) University, politicians turned their eyes to the vast west ruled under charter by the Hudson's Bay Company. At the time, the company's effectiveness as a governing body was slipping badly. Free traders were challenging its monopoly. American interests were speculating on the possibility that the United States might be able to annex the territory if the HBC's charter was revoked. A steady trickle of newcomers, many from Upper Canada, was swelling the population of the area. In particular, many settled in the valleys of the Red and Assiniboine Rivers where, despite the number of migrants, the population was still dominated by the Métis nation.

Although there was a small British garrison of regular soldiers at Fort Garry in the 1850s, the real "military" in the Red River Valley was that connected to the highly organized Métis buffalo hunt, a semi-annual expedition to the plains west of the Red River. The large numbers of people involved in the hunt, the complexity of the preparations, and the operation of its mobile camps called for self-imposed discipline that had evolved over many generations. Several contemporary historians have referred to the Métis "cavalry" as being the next best thing to a military force.

Dr. John Schultz arrived in Red River about 1861. Physicians were in short supply and there was a demand for his services, but he, being a man of great ambition and acquisitiveness, soon launched into a variety of enterprises. He traded in furs, opened a store, and become involved in—and virtual leader of—the Canadian Party, a group whose aim was to end the HBC monopoly and bring about the annexation of Rupert's Land by Canada.

In 1864 and 1865 Schultz bought the settlement's first newspaper, the *Nor'-Wester*, as a propaganda medium. The *Nor'-Wester* thus became bitterly critical of the HBC and painted glowing pictures of the future that lay ahead if the company's territory was to become part of Canada.

During the 1860s a state close to anarchy developed in the Red River Settlement. A local council developed at Portage la Prairie and a public meeting demanded the formation of a provisional government to fill the vacuum created by the disintegration of the HBC's authority. Schultz was in the forefront of the growing agitation for a Canadian takeover.

To make matters more involved, nobody in the HBC, the Canadian government, or the British government thought to tell the people of Red River about the progress in negotiations to take over the territory from the company. The only news that got through was that which appeared in the *Nor'-Wester*, and that was definitely slanted. The Métis had long held land along both the rivers, mostly in long narrow river lots similar to those in Quebec along the St. Lawrence River. Caught up in the conflicting rumours and the biased reports in the *Nor'-Wester*, the Métis were confused and fearful that they would lose their traditional land and customs.

In 1869 plans were made by the new Dominion of Canada to take over the HBC holdings. Ottawa appointed a governor for the new territory, and the chosen official, William McDougall, set about having a survey conducted. Meanwhile the building of the Dawson Trail was authorized, and McDougall started west through the United States to proclaim his authority.

The Métis responded to fragmentary reports of these plans by stopping the survey, halting McDougall at the United States border, and forming a committee, with a number of European supporters, along the lines of the buffalo hunt organization.

Schultz and his Canadian Party immediately denounced the Métis action as armed rebellion and put together a counter force. Several attempts at a compromise were made, but Schultz refused the Métis access to much-needed stores of food stockpiled for the Dawson Trail crews. In a settlement where two bad years had produced widespread hardship, Schultz's denial of supplies was tantamount to a declaration of war.

The food was stored in Schultz's house near Upper Fort Garry. The Canadian Party barricaded itself in the house and defied the Métis, who surrounded the building and brought up a cannon from the fort.

Even the most dedicated of partisans could not have any answer for such an action except surrender. Schultz and his colleagues were imprisoned in the Upper Fort. In a few days, however, his wife smuggled a gimlet to him and, with this and a rope made of buffalo robe strips, Schultz escaped through a window. But the gimlet to which he had anchored the rope pulled out of the window frame and Schultz fell, injuring himself severely. In spite of that, he dragged himself to the home of a neutral settler who sheltered him out of compassion until he escaped to the south and then to Ontario.

In Ontario, Schultz lost no time in arousing opinion against the "rebels" of the Red River. Between his efforts and the execution of Thomas Scott at Fort Garry, many Ontarians developed a vengeful and intolerant attitude towards the Métis and their provisional government.

After Manitoba had been admitted into Confederation in 1870, Schultz was one of the first Members of Parliament elected by the new province. He held a seat from 1871 to 1882, then moved up to the Senate until 1888. Shortly after that, he was knighted and appointed lieutenant-governor of Manitoba, a post he held until 1895. He died in Monterey, Mexico, in 1896.

A big man at six-foot-four, he cut a wide swath in Manitoba politics and was either greatly admired or thoroughly disliked. Colonel C. A.

Boulton, a colleague from the Canadian Party days, wrote: "Dr. Schultz is an able and in many ways a remarkable man. Possessed of a magnificent physique and great force of character, he was popular in the cause he espoused and was a tower of strength to it."

However, Sir John A. Macdonald, in a letter to John Ross about the problems encountered by the 1869 surveyors, wrote: "I am afraid they fraternized too much with that fellow Schultz, who is a clever sort of a man but extremely cantankerous and ill-conditioned."

A Tale of Two Tourists

*The two tourists, Viscount Milton and Dr. Cheadle, with
Métis guide Louis Battenotte, known as "the Assiniboine,"
with his Cree wife to the right and their son to the left.*

In the nineteenth century, western Canada was not exactly a tourism hotspot. Pleasure excursions to the frontier required no small amount of effort on the part of travellers. Still, there were many who took their chances in the hopes of learning more about the New World and returning home with a fantastic tale or two to tell.

Walter Butler Cheadle, age twenty-six, was a newly graduated English doctor when he decided in 1862 to come to western Canada "for pleasure," to see new lands, hunt buffalo, and visit the Cariboo gold fields. He was accompanied by William Fitzwilliam, Viscount Milton, age twenty-two, who suffered numerous ailments and proved to be one of the many difficulties Cheadle experienced during his trip.

They left Liverpool aboard the liner *Anglo-Saxon* and landed at Quebec City. From there they travelled by boat to Toronto, by rail through Chicago to La Crosse on the Mississippi, by steamboat to St. Paul, Minnesota, by rail to St. Anthony, by stage to Georgetown, and then partway down the Red River until they were picked up by the sternwheeler *International*.

Cheadle's party arrived at the Red and Assiniboine junction on 7 August, and in his diary Cheadle noted that "The Fort [is] very superior to Albercrombie or Georgetown [in the United States]; good stone wall enclosure flanked by round towers; portholes glazed; offices, store and governor's house inside . . . Good white houses, settlement 20 or 30 miles along River [sic]. Nunnery. Hudson's Bay store always full; pretty good port and sherry."

Although there was a doctor in the settlement, Cheadle found his professional skills in great demand. He was taken to see several patients and treated them during his stay. He called at the post office, the printing office, and the office of the *Nor'-Wester*. In addition, he found several people who had been all the way to the mountains and noted in his diary some of their experiences, particularly with "grisly" bears.

Cheadle's initial intention was for his expedition to go for a one-month buffalo hunt west of Fort Garry and to depart for the Saskatchewan

River area after that. But they decided they didn't have enough time for the buffalo hunt, so they started to gather equipment for their long journey west.

"Things at Fort stores dear," Cheadle noted, as he listed and ordered his supplies. He ordered 300 pounds (136 kg) of flour, 100 pounds (45 kg) of pemmican, 8 gallons (30 L) of rum, 20 pounds (9 kg) of tobacco, powder, shot, musket balls, a blanket, a buffalo robe, tea, coffee, salt, pepper, duffle cloth, and one pair of "beaverteen trousers." He bought twelve pairs of moccasins, a caribou skin hunting shirt, a pair of mooseskin breeches, and leggings.

They had quite a time buying horses and had to pay as much as thirty English pounds for a good horse. The guides and men of the party were hired and with each a contract was signed. Pay was from six to twelve pounds a month, with advances that the men left with their families.

Since Cheadle and Milton were sleeping in a tent outside the fort to help them get accustomed to the life, they found the mosquitoes almost unbearable. One night, as Cheadle wrote in his journals, they "made a small fire in a hole in the ground inside the tent when it had burned up well, placed sods over; filled the tent with smoke and kept in till morning, effectually settling the mosquitoes." That day, however, black flies made their appearance, and they were forced to light fires near their horses to protect them from those insects.

A few days before the party left, they called on the Anglican bishop, Bishop Anderson. Cheadle wrote: "Walked to the Fort, called on McTavish & borrowed 2 horses on which we rode to the [bishop's] palace, a little square white house well furnished, untidy garden like all the others. Bishop and sister plain homely people, very kind; stayed tea; talked over English news. Returned home after dark."

On 18 August Cheadle met another English group who had come to do some hunting along the South Saskatchewan River. Lord Dunmore, Colonel Cowper, and Captain Thynne were going after buffalo and grizzly bears. Afterward, there was a final visit to Bishop Anderson, where Cheadle had turkey, veal, beef, and two bottles of port, and he met the new judge, a Mr. Black. He added in his diary: "Stayed rather late. Lord M. [Milton] sits with Miss La Ronde until 1 AM fixing hunting shirt."

Finally they departed from the fort on 23 August at 4 PM and camped at Sturgeon Creek, 15 kilometres (9 mi.) away. Cheadle wrote: "Called in to see Mr. Rowand. Stout man. Pretty, white wood house picked out with green. Garden. Best place we have seen at Red River Settlement. New feeling, riding alongside caravan."

Between Fort Garry and the trading post near present Portage la Prairie, they encountered a Métis wedding, and some of the men found all sorts of excuses to stop for the night. Cheadle wrote:

Great number of guests. Two fiddlers; dance a cross between lancers and quadrille; much double shuffle. Bride very pretty, pensive-looking. Lord M. dances. Get him away with difficulty. Voudrie, cousin of bride, swears there is no water for 15 miles and we must camp there till next day as the horses were done! Find the men at the Fort ¼ mile further on; all say no more to be done that day. Lots of drunken half-breeds collect round us & insist on treating us to corn whisky . . . On the way in the morning, Milton & Messiter quarrel tremendously & threaten to fight. I ride between and expostulate, quieten down. La Ronde rather sulky penitent.

Cheadle's diary for 29 August notes: "In Indian territory after leaving the last Fort [Portage] & have seen the last of houses for many a day." They wintered near Fort Carlton in some discomfort, then moved on to Edmonton, from which they entered the mountains and endured severe hardships. They were saved from complete disaster only by the "indomitable spirit and resources of their French half-breed guide, Louis Battenotte."

They reached Kamloops, then Victoria, and returned to England via San Francisco and New York.

After their harrowing experiences in Canada, Cheadle and Milton were content, it appears, to settle down in England. Cheadle became well known as a surgeon and made children's health his chief interest. In spite of a great deal of opposition from medical colleagues, he strongly supported women's rights to practice medicine and was one of the earliest professors to conduct lectures for women at the London School of Medicine. He died in 1910.

"For God's Sake Men, Don't Fire! I Have a Wife and Family!"

Thomas Spence, who hid under the table when shots were fired in his courtroom, is seen here, at the extreme right, as a member of Riel's Council.

Thanks to Saturday-morning cartoons and the National Film Board of Canada, a generation of Canadian children in the 1970s and 1980s learned how the short-lived "Republic of Manitobah" ended in a brawl. But there is far more to the story than that.

Thomas Spence arrived in Portage la Prairie in 1867 from England by way of Montreal and Fort Garry. In Montreal he had worked with a group of engineers who were renovating the fortifications at Point Levis. When he arrived in the little settlement south of Lake Manitoba, he opened a general store. Almost immediately, he became involved in politics.

"The Portage," as it was then called, lay outside the area centered on Fort Garry and governed by the Council of Assiniboia, a somewhat ineffectual body set up by the Hudson's Bay Company in response to a growing demand for a greater voice in their own government by the population of the settlement at the junction of the Red and Assiniboine Rivers.

At that time, the Portage-area settlers had organized a local council at the suggestion of Anglican minister, William Cockran. This council had no real authority except the consent of the residents of the district, but it was functioning quite well when Thomas Spence appeared and was, in a short time, elected a member of the council.

Characterized by historian W. L. Morton as "a man of some education, intelligent but romantic and conceited," Spence had large ideas about the nature and role of the governing body to which he had been named. As a first step toward creating the west's first truly representative government, he prevailed on his fellow councillors to reorganize the structure of the body and create the office of president—to which he was immediately elected.

The boundaries of this new authority were to be the United States border on the south, Lake Manitoba on the north, the hundredth meridian (where Brandon is now) on the west, and the boundary of Assiniboia on the east (where High Bluff is now).

The first name chosen for this new entity was Caledonia, but this was later changed to the Government of Manitoba, in recognition of Manitou, the Great Spirit of the Plains Indians. Constituencies were laid out and taxes and tariffs were imposed to finance the new government. Numerous writers have used the term "republic" to describe this regime and have also insisted that the spelling *Manitobah* be used. A final "h" may well have been added in some versions of the authority's name because, even then, some place names varied in spelling.

The council set about establishing its legal status by writing to the Colonial Office in London on 19 February 1868 to gain recognition by the Crown. On 30 May, London replied that British subjects could set up a local government for municipal purposes but could not go any further without the approval of the Crown.

However, Spence and his colleagues had already levied tariffs on imports and had notified all those trading in imported goods. Among these was the manager of the Hudson's Bay Company post who declared he would pay no duties unless they were authorized by the government of Rupert's Land—which was, of course, the HBC. According to the *Free Press* of 9 October 1890, the council "decided it couldn't force him to pay, but could make it hot for him when the gaol [jail] was built."

This was not the only case of defying the council. A shoemaker named Macpherson, who lived at High Bluff on the border of Assiniboia, was heard to remark that the taxes being imposed were not for the jail but for liquor and beer for the councillors. For this, he was branded as "obnoxious to the president and council" and a warrant for his arrest on a charge of treason was issued. Constables William Hudson and Henry Anderson were sent to bring in the dissident "dead or alive." They are, according to the records, suspected of having imbibed enough to make their approach to Macpherson's house a noisy one.

On entering Macpherson's home, Hudson found the shoemaker cleaning his revolver. He produced the warrant and tried, single-handed, to get Macpherson out. Anderson then took part in the scuffle, during which Macpherson broke free and ran toward the Assiniboia boundary. The constables overtook him on horseback. They then commandeered a jumper—a small, one-horse open sleigh—and were transporting him to the Portage when they met John and Aleck McLean, a father and son returning from work.

The McLeans later described seeing a man—Macpherson—jump from the sleigh. His clothes were torn, they said, and he had to hold his trousers up with one hand as he tried to escape, calling to them for help. The McLeans would have come to his aid but they were confronted by the constables and the warrant and stood back. However, they followed the trio to the settlement.

The constables took their prisoner to a warehouse, which was jammed with people interested in the ensuing trial. The McLeans picked up three friends—Bob Hastie, Yankee Johnston, and Mr. Chapman—and were able to get into the warehouse where Spence, as judge, sat at one end of a table with Macpherson at the other end.

John McLean asked what crime Macpherson was charged with. Spence replied, "Treason against the laws of the government."

McLean replied, "Ye have no laws. Who is the accuser?"

A constable said, "Mr. Spence."

Said McLean in his thick Scottish brogue, "Come oot o'that, ye whited sepulchre; ye canna act as judge and accuser both."

Hudson then ordered John McLean to leave, which McLean agreed to do since it was Hudson's property on which the trial was being held. But Hastie, when he saw Hudson and Anderson move to follow McLean outside and fearing they would rough him up, shouted, "Ye're no goin' oot there alone," and grabbed Macpherson.

A general melee broke out, with one or more shots fired into the roof. Everyone rushed out via doors and windows, but John McLean returned a few moments later and found Thomas Spence under the table, shouting, "For God's sake men, don't fire! I have a wife and family!"

At least, that's the way several contemporary observers described it, as well as the National Film Board of Canada in its 1978 *Canada Vignette* entitled *Spence's Republic*, which was a staple on Canadian TV for a generation.

Macpherson's trial went no further, and the fledgling government of Manitoba ended in a welter of shouts, shots, and general confusion.

Spence and his colleagues were discredited men, but the original local council, which he had tried to enhance, resumed its unassuming and limited functions until Manitoba became a province two years later.

Most authoritative writers deny there was any attempt to set up a state totally independent of Rupert's Land, or of Britain. The letter to the Colonial Office would never have been written by a group of revolutionary republicans. Spence and his friends were loyalists seeking only a measure of self-government with, admittedly, a good measure of self-aggrandizement.

The embarrassing end of "Manitobah" did not stop Spence. He later became clerk of the Manitoba Legislature, census commissioner for the North-Western Territory, immigration agent for Canada in California, and, finally, assistant registrar in the Edmonton land titles office.

He died in Edmonton on 19 March 1900, a respected civil servant whose memories must surely have included some bitter feelings about a dream shattered by a couple of independent-minded Scotsmen.

What Election Rules?

Thomas Greenway led the Liberals to the first true party government in Manitoba, in 1888.

When Manitobans go to the polls to elect their next legislative assembly, their numbers will be many times greater than those who voted in the first provincial election in December 1870.

At that time Manitoba was a much smaller province with a population of a mere 11,963. Of these, 5,757 were listed as Métis, 4,083 as English half-breeds, 558 as Indians, and 1,565 as whites. The division along religious lines was 6,247 Catholics versus 5,716 Protestants. By comparison, the list of qualified electors today is nearly 733,000, with the northernmost constituency running along the western shore of Hudson Bay.

The legislature currently numbers fifty-seven members. In 1870 there were twenty-four seats in the assembly, and the constituencies were carefully planned so that members would include equal numbers of francophones and anglophones.

Modern parliamentary tradition decrees that the leader of the largest party in the legislature becomes premier and forms a government. In the first few years of Manitoba's existence, there were no political parties, and Adams Archibald, the first lieutenant-governor, had to play it by ear. In fact some authorities claim that Archibald was his own premier because there was no one in the legislature with the experience needed to administer the province.

From 1870 to 1874, four men served as the lieutenant-governor's chief adviser, which is what the premier is supposed to be. This list included H. J. H. Clarke, Alfred Boyd, N. A. Girard, and R. A. Davis who was, incidentally, proprietor of one of Winnipeg's first hotels.

Davis stayed in office for two years and was succeeded by his principal supporter, John Norquay. Manitoba's first native-born head of government and first mixed-blood premier, Norquay held a precarious majority together until 1878. He was premier until 1887, followed by the year-long tenure of D. H. Harrison.

Even though parties as we know them scarcely existed for the first few years of Manitoba's history, partisan feelings were strong if based on personalities. Speeches ran for hours, meetings would drag on all night, and frequently feelings ran so high that participants in political gatherings often ran out of arguments and patience at about the same time and came to blows.

One writer described an election meeting attended by citizens hostile to the principal speaker: "They attended in force, abundantly supplied with eggs of an uncertain age. By the time they got through with their work, none of the occupants of the platform was recognizable." The target of those eggs was Donald A. Smith, later Lord Strathcona.

Smith, who was a power in the Hudson's Bay Company, the Bank of Montreal, and the Canadian Pacific Railway, was then a member of both the provincial legislature of Manitoba and of the House of Commons—you could sit in both houses in those days.

The first true party government in Manitoba came into office in 1888, when Thomas Greenway's Liberals won a majority of seats in the legislature. Greenway came from Ontario and had led a considerable party of settlers west to Manitoba where they took up land in the southwestern part of the province and founded several towns, including Crystal City.

Greenway's first term of office ended the CPR's monopoly on railway operation in the west. This was cause for much jubilation, as Manitobans—farmers especially—felt very strongly that the CPR was charging far too much for poor service and wanted to see competing lines challenging the original railway's claims to protection.

Greenway was also responsible for two acts that had national repercussions and produced complications that are unsettled to this day. These were the Manitoba School Act of 1890, which established the public school system and denied tax revenue to church schools, and the Language Act of 1890, which was intended to cancel out the 1870 Manitoba Act guarantee of language rights for the French.

During the First World War, a major scandal over the building of the Legislative Building resulted in the downfall of Sir Rodmond Roblin's Conservative government. The Liberal government under T. C. Norris, which followed Roblin's, lost its steam after its first term and left the electors frustrated and adventurous.

In the 1921 election, the Norris government was re-elected, but as a minority. There were also Conservatives, Farmer, Labour, and independent MLAs in the legislature. When a new election was called in 1922, the United Farmers won twenty-seven of the fifty-four seats. The Liberals won seven, Conservatives six, Labour six, and independents eight. The leaderless United Farmers group persuaded John Bracken, then principal of the Manitoba Agricultural College, to become premier, even though he had no experience in politics and indeed no seat in the legislature.

Bracken was premier until 1942 and the United Farmers won majorities in 1927 and 1932. In 1931 the provincial Liberals joined Bracken's government in a coalition and were given three cabinet seats in what was, for all intents and purposes, a Liberal-Progressive government. In 1936 the effects of the Depression were felt in the provincial voting, with Bracken's government winning only twenty-two seats, and with Conservatives taking sixteen, Co-operative Commonwealth Federation (CCF) six, Social Credit five, independents three, and Communists one.

In 1936 Bracken was again in a minority position. He negotiated the support of Social Credit MLAs, though none of them entered the cabinet, and managed to hang on until 1940, when the need for a united front within the province to deal with federal-provincial relations became apparent. A coalition government was formed under Bracken, with Conservatives and CCF members in the cabinet, and this administration got strong voter support in the December 1940 election.

After Bracken left to lead the national Conservative Party (forcing it to add the word Progressive to its name), Stuart Garson became premier and led the coalition, now minus the CCF, to another victory in 1945. Garson was succeeded in 1948 by Douglas Campbell, one of the original 1922 United Farmer MLAs and the first native-born Manitoban since Norquay to lead a government. He won majorities in 1949 and 1953, although by the latter date the Conservatives had withdrawn from the coalition, leaving the government in the hands of Liberal-Progressive members.

Another minority government occurred in 1958, when Duff Roblin's Conservatives won twenty-six seats, while Campbell's ranks numbered only nineteen and the CCF's eleven. The next year Roblin won a majority in a new election and retained power in the 1962 and 1966 elections, albeit with reduced majorities.

The minority pattern was repeated in 1969, when Ed Schreyer's New Democratic Party (successors to the CCF) were the biggest party in the legislature but lacked a majority. With Liberal support, they stayed in office through the 1973 election, when they finally won a majority.

Manitoba voters have continued to alternate between Conservative and NDP provincial governments ever since, electing Progressive Conservative Sterling Lyon in 1977, the NDP's Howard Pawley in 1981, Progressive Conservative Gary Filmon in 1988, and NDP leader Gary Doer in 1999.

One peculiarity about Manitoba politics is that, during the 1920s, 1930s, and 1940s, members of the legislature were elected by a system known as proportional representation, in which voters gave candidates a number indicating their preference. Number one, of course, was the voter's first choice, then numbers two, three, and four in descending order of preference. A quota, the equivalent of fifty per cent of the votes cast plus one, was set in each constituency and if the candidate with the highest number of votes didn't reach that quota, the low candidate was dropped and his second choices distributed. This went on until a candidate reached the required quota.

Proportional representation was also used in municipal elections, but was dropped during the Duff Roblin years in favour of the first-past-the-post system, in which the winner may represent a minority of the electors.

Icelanders Survive on the Frontier

The first Icelandic settlers arrive at Willow Point on Lake Winnipeg, approximately 1.6 kilometres (1 mi.) south of the present town of Gimli, in October 1875.

MANITOBA ARCHIVES (ICELANDIC SETTLEMENT 2)

The first Icelandic settlers to come to Manitoba—didn't. They set up their colony of New Iceland in an area that is part of Manitoba now, but wasn't then. At that time Manitoba was a "postage stamp" province, with its northern boundary ending just north of present-day Winnipeg Beach.

The initial group of Icelandic immigrants to Manitoba didn't come from Iceland, either, or at least not directly. Icelandic interest in North America was first aroused in 1870, and the first to leave their island in the Atlantic came to the United States and Ontario. However, the Ontario group was dissatisfied with the conditions they faced northwest of Toronto and started looking for a better place to settle. In July 1875 the group sent a delegation to investigate the land around Winnipeg.

Because many of the Icelanders were fishermen, the delegation chose land about 58 kilometres (36 mi.) along the shore from the then-Manitoba boundary to north of what is now the Icelandic River (including what is now Hecla Island) and 16 kilometres (10 mi.) inland.

Ottawa was cool to the idea of an Icelandic settlement near Manitoba until Governor General Lord Dufferin came to the Icelanders' aide. An admirer of things Icelandic since his visit to the island in 1856, a journey that he related in his book, *Letters from High Latitudes*, he persuaded the federal authorities to grant the land that was to become New Iceland.

Travelling through the United States and down the Red River on a sternwheeler, the party of 285 reached Winnipeg on 11 October 1875. They decided that the first town they would build would be called Gimli, after the home of the gods in Old Norse legends.

Some fifty decided to stay in Winnipeg to work (see sidebar, "Icelanders Left Their Mark on Winnipeg"), and the rest landed in their new home on 21 October. Although the weather was good, they decided that moving north to the preferred location on the Icelandic River was not feasible, and they set about cutting trees for log cabins for winter shelter.

Although the group included some sixty families, there were only enough stoves available for thirty houses, so many families had to double

Icelanders Left Their Mark on Winnipeg

Of the nearly three hundred Icelandic immigrants who came west in 1875 about fifty remained in Winnipeg. Those who stayed in the city immediately looked for work. Men sought employment in cargo handling and wood sawing; women looked for domestic work.

The men who set up as wood sawyers did so as independent self-employed workers. They equipped themselves with axes, bucksaws, and sawhorses and, carrying these items, went about the small city, offering to saw, split, and pile cordwood they noticed stacked in backyards. Others manhandled goods and materials arriving or departing on the river steamers, or cut and loaded the huge quantities of wood the ships required.

The women and girls, many of whom quickly gained reputations as good cooks, could earn about eight dollars a month in domestic service if they spoke English.

The Icelanders who stayed in Winnipeg were joined, for short periods of time, by people from the Gimli area, who looked for work there during breakup or when work on the land was impossible. Some landed jobs on railway construction gangs building the CPR line toward the city from the east, at pay rates of fifteen cents an hour or a dollar-fifty a day. Others signed on as deckhands on the river and lake boats, the forty-dollar monthly pay being fairly good for the time.

The first Icelander to build a home in Winnipeg was Fridrik Sigurbjörnsson, who built on what was then known as the Hudson Bay Flats. Sigurbjörnsson and Sigrid Jonsdottir became the first Icelandic couple to be married in Winnipeg on 6 September 1876.

At first the homes built by Ice-landic "squatters" on the flats were little better than shanties made from scrap lumber and various other materials at hand. The Brown and Rutherford sawmill was located nearby and was of considerable help to the people as they built shelters. Within a few years, however, these crude dwellings had been replaced by better structures. As more Icelanders arrived, the demand for accommodation grew. A few obtained homes in Point Douglas, which many looked upon as a prestigious community. Icelandic boarding houses were started by Jon Thordarson on Graham Avenue and by Gisli Johnson at Henry Avenue and Main Street. Thordarson's house was known as Icelandic House and was a social and cultural centre for the Icelandic community in the city.

The need to learn English was a primary concern for these newcomers and, as early as 1876–77, a number of them organized an English class with Magnus Paulson as instructor. By 1879 there were six Icelandic students attending the two-room school at the corner of Carlton Street and Notre Dame Avenue and, although there were some accounts of prejudice against them by other pupils, the Icelanders were fairly soon accepted.

For a couple of years there were no resident Icelandic clergymen in Manitoba, and homes on the flats were the scene of spontaneous gatherings for worship conducted by laymen. Reverend Jon Bjarnason held the first service in Icelandic on 21 October 1877 in Grace Methodist Church.

The Winnipeg Icelanders formed the Icelandic Society, later the Icelandic National Society of America, in 1877. Its aim was "to preserve and promote the honour of the Icelandic people . . . and

---

Icelanders Left Their Mark on Winnipeg (cont.)

to preserve and cultivate that liberal and progressive spirit of culture which has throughout the ages characterized the Icelandic people." The society kept track of Icelanders in Canada, promoted a Sunday school, aided the sick and destitute, and supported the Icelandic newspaper, Framfari, started in Riverton in 1877.

Dances, card playing, and music were the chief recreations of the Icelanders in those early years. A choral group and a dramatic society were formed, and, in 1880, a full-length play, Sigrid, Son of Eyjatford, was offered in Icelandic.

The first Icelandic merchant to open a business was Arni Frederickson, who came to Winnipeg in 1875. He was unable to do outside work, having been disabled as a result of freezing his feet. But he worked for a time in a Toronto shoe factory and, in 1879, opened a shoe repair shop and store near City Hall on Main Street.

In the boom years of 1880–82, an Icelandic investment company entered the wild real estate speculation of the era. But like many other such enterprises, it collapsed when the boom burst.

By the end of the first five years of their settlement, there were close to eight hundred Icelanders in the city, and they had made their mark on the community.

---

up. Fishing proved to be a disappointment, largely because of unsuitable equipment, and despite a federal grant of five thousand dollars, supplies ran short. Scurvy appeared, taking several lives.

In spite of the difficult weather and strange conditions, the Icelanders found time and energy to set up classes for their children. They also formed a local government despite the lack of any arrangements for such a development in the North-Western Territory. They asked Ottawa for a survey and roads.

Twelve hundred new arrivals came from Iceland in the summer of 1876 after the eruption of volcanoes there buried 6,475 square kilometres (2,500 sq. mi.) of populated land with a thick layer of ash and pumice. Unused as they were to heavily wooded land, they found the clearing of their farms very difficult, and their work was complicated by lack of roads, distance, and the weather, which became bitter early in October. During that summer, however, the federal government provided funds for a road to Netley, a project on which many of the settlers obtained work at sixty or seventy cents a day, plus board.

The winter of 1876–77 brought one of the greatest crises in the struggling settlement's young history when smallpox broke out near Riverton in September. By mid-winter almost every home in Gimli was affected. Calls for medical aid were sent to Winnipeg, and three doctors—David Young, James Lynch, and A. Baldwin—opened a hospital using the government storehouse.

The colony was quarantined. Anyone coming south from Gimli was required to stop at Netley Creek, to wait fifteen days, to bathe, and to get clean clothing. Supplies intended for the settlement were dumped in the snow at or near Netley Creek, and food began to run very low in the homes of New Iceland. There were forty deaths in December; in all, the disease took over a hundred lives, and almost half the people in the settlement contracted it.

The epidemic faded away in April, but the quarantine remained. In July several hundred settlers mustered at Gimli, without weapons, but determined to force their way through the Netley checkpost. On 20 July, the quarantine was lifted.

Gradually, with the aid of a government loan, the settlers resumed their struggle against the wilderness and their efforts to learn new ways of farming, fishing, and living.

In the midst of the ravaging epidemic, they found the strength to draw up a constitution for the good government of their settlement and, a little later in 1877, to found a newspaper, *Framfari*. Even before the quarantine ended, Icelanders debated the question of obtaining the services of a pastor and setting up a church.

Classes that were started for the children in 1876 were suspended during the worst of the epidemic but, as soon as the doctors said it was safe, they reopened the school, with an enrolment of sixty-three.

Greasepaint and Spotlights

*The Province Theatre, in 1922, was one of the many theatres
in Winnipeg at the height of the theatre and vaudeville era.*

ARCHIVES OF MANITOBA (N2717)

Back in the days before movies, television, and the Internet, there was only live theatre—real people acting and speaking on stages before live audiences. Live theatre provided entertainment and escape to Manitoba's early residents and was an important part of its cultural landscape.

There was no tradition of live theatre among Manitoba's first Selkirk settlers because such a thing didn't exist in the remote and rural highlands and islands of Scotland from whence they came. It wasn't until 26 December 1870 that Winnipeg's first dramatic presentation was offered by the 10th Ontario Rifles Music and Drama Association. The play was *The Child of Circumstance* and was performed in the Theatre Royal in the Bannatyne Building. The first locally written and produced play was *The Outlaws*, presented by the Icelandic Drama Company in 1885.

By 1890 a substantial brick building on Notre Dame Avenue was proclaimed the Winnipeg Opera House, and a few years later the American impresario Corless Powers Walker built the Walker Theatre. The theatre opened in 1907 with its first performance, Puccini's *Madam Butterfly*. The Walker was acclaimed as one of the finest theatres in North America, with excellent acoustics, a richly decorated interior, and the latest in backstage equipment. This building still exists. From 1945 to 1990 it was the Odeon Theatre. In 1990 it returned to a stage theatre and is now the Burton Cummings Centre for the Performing Arts.

The latter part of the nineteenth century brought performers from the various vaudeville circuits, who presented songs, dances, comedy skits, jugglers, illusionists, acrobats, and comedians of widely varying artistic ability, and—we may be sure—received equally varying receptions by audiences. Many vaudeville artists who later became Hollywood legends did their thing in Winnipeg—W. C. Fields, Buster Keaton, Harold Lloyd, and even Charlie Chaplin, to name a few. World-famous singers and musicians also gave concerts in the city's theatres.

Visiting dramatic actors and actresses made stops in Winnipeg, offering a wide variety of plays and talents. Sir Henry Irving, an outstanding English actor of the pre–First World War period, supported by his wife,

A Night at the Movies

The first motion pictures in the form of nickelodeons were shown in Winnipeg in 1899 in a tent close to where the old Starland Theatre was located.

Although many movie palaces were constructed in Winnipeg in the first few decades of the twentieth century, sadly, virtually all of these grand structures have been swept away by the march of city development. Yet, for decades, going to the movies was a great event, long before the advent of multiplexes rendered a night at the movies a sterile, assembly-line affair.

Before motion pictures could "talk," every movie theatre in Winnipeg had a pianist who played throughout the feature films, using music selected to fit the mood of the drama unfolding on the screen. Some theatres, such as the Garrick and the Capitol, had magnificent pipe organs that were played at intermission.

In the two decades or so after the arrival of "Talkies," all movie houses provided a pretty full program, including a ninety-minute (or so) feature film, a newsreel, a short comedy, and a cartoon. Sometimes the comedy was replaced with a travelogue that inevitably ended with the narrator speaking such words as: "as the sun slowly sinks into the west, we leave this beauty spot of the South Pacific [or Caribbean, or Mediterranean]."

Saturday matinees were famous

for the noise generated by many children from the ages of four to fourteen. Parents simply gave their offspring the nickel or dime for a movie ticket and sent them to the show. The doors opened about half an hour before the program started, and the theatre was quickly filled with shouting, arguing, running, popcorn-eating kids who often had to be silenced by the theatre manager who would threaten to cancel the show.

Matinee programs included features specially chosen for kids and a cartoon, a short comedy (such as Our Gang *or* Buster Keaton*), and a serial that ran for six to twelve weeks. The serial always included good guys and bad guys, easily identifiable, who went through incredible adventures. Each installment always left the good guys in dire peril from crocodiles, buzz saws, approaching locomotives, lethal snakes, or burning buildings. Only in the final segment did good triumph, even though in every one of the perilous installments, excited young voices from the audience warned the endangered heroes or heroines on the screen of approaching doom.*

The atmosphere of the old movie houses made one feel like a welcomed and privileged guest for whom the management had provided surroundings that were, if not luxurious, at least made to look it.

Ellen Terry, played the Walker on several occasions.

An enduring record of the couple's last appearance appears in a brass plaque in the lobby of the Walker (later Odeon) Theatre, commemorating the fact that Winnipeg was their last performance before they met their deaths by drowning in 1912 when the passenger liner *Empress of Ireland* sank in the Gulf of St. Lawrence.

Always welcomed in Winnipeg were the touring companies of the

Shakespeare Theatre at Stratford-on-Avon, the Abbey Theatre of Dublin, and the D'Oyly Carte Opera Company from England.

The Stratford group specialized, naturally, in the plays of William Shakespeare, breathing life and fire into what many Winnipeg youths had regarded in school as dull exercises in their English courses. Macbeth murdered Duncan, Henry V inspired his outnumbered soldiers before the Battle of Agincourt, and Romeo and Juliet followed their star-crossed destiny before the eyes of enthralled patrons.

Ireland's troubles and the endearing and infuriating characteristics of the Irish were portrayed by the Abbey Theatre Players in the works of J. M. Synge, Lord Dunsany, Sean O'Casey, and Lady Gregory. Meanwhile, the foibles and contradictions of English life were parodied by the D'Oyly Carte.

For a short time after the First World War, a company called the Dumbbells played Winnipeg on several occasions. This was an entertainment group put together from talented members of the Canadian military during the war. For a few years they were regular visitors to Winnipeg, with their songs and skits about the war and their sometimes funny, sometimes sardonic representations of military life.

There were also homegrown groups that played the city that were usually formed with the inspiration and effort of one or two leading personalities. Such groups included the Winnipeg Little Theatre (WLT), formed in the early 1920s, which followed a policy of producing annual full-length dramatic shows. The group managed to obtain a former movie theatre where Selkirk Avenue joins Main Street. Extensive alterations were made to create a stage, lighting, flies for scenery, and rather primitive dressing-room facilities.

The personnel of the WLT changed over the years, but many people who later made their mark in stage, radio, and film started off in Winnipeg with the WLT. Arnie Eggertson, for example, played in and directed WLT shows even as he starred in Icelandic community dramas and in the Progressive Players' productions. A man of great sincerity and ability, his taste ran to the tragic, and a fellow actor once remarked of him that, "he's never happier than when he's saddest."

Douglas Rain, another WLT alumnus and a Winnipeg native, would go on to film immortality as the voice of the HAL 9000 computer in Stanley Kubrick's classic film *2001: A Space Odyssey*. Others connected with the WLT were Tommy Tweed, Winston McQuillan, Lady Margot Tupper, and

Moray Sinclair, who later was the moving spirit behind the formation of the Masquers' Club, comprised largely of Eaton's employees.

Another Winnipeg-based group was the Progressive Players. As the name implied, its members were left leaning politically, and some of its productions were intended to carry a social or political message. Consisting mostly of one-act plays, the Progressive Players' programs mixed comedy and propaganda and were presented in a number of rural communities. James and Mabel Aiken were the spark plugs of this group, which operated for more than a decade in the late 1920s and 1930s.

The 1930s, years of depression, were good years for plays with social content. One such feature, *Eight Men Speak Out*, was based on the trial of eight Canadians for Communist activity and was banned in both Winnipeg and Toronto. Another well-known drama, *Waiting for Lefty*, was presented at the Walker Theatre in the mid-1930s, with Joe Zuken as one of the leading characters. Zuken was also involved in a dramatization of Sinclair Lewis's novel, *It Can't Happen Here*, about a Fascist takeover in the United States.

One of the major developments in local theatre occurred in 1957 when Tom Hendry founded Theatre 77, which combined the following year with the WLT to form the Manitoba Theatre Centre. Closely associated with Hendry in this venture was John Hirsch, who went on to an outstanding career at Stratford, Ontario, and in the CBC Drama Department.

No story of drama in Winnipeg would be complete without mention of Le Cercle Molière, a French-language group that mounted many presentations of both classical and modern French plays and competed successfully for what was at one time the top award in Canadian amateur drama, the Bessborough Trophy. This was established in 1932 by Governor General Lord Bessborough and was competed for annually until 1970.

Winnipeg made its mark on one of the greatest entertainers in history. Bob Hope, veteran of vaudeville, film, and television, was rarely photographed without a golf club in his hand. After he passed away in the summer of 2003, it was remembered that he learned to play the game when he was taken to a Winnipeg golf course to kill time between matinee and evening performances during a visit to the city.

Riverboats Ran Desperate Races

The steamboat International, *one of the boats known to have participated in races and the one on which an unsolved murder occurred, is seen here at the* HBC *warehouse at Upper Fort Garry, in 1872.*

In the late 1850s and early 1860s, there were many opinions about what would happen to the vast region of Canada controlled by the Hudson's Bay Company once its long reign finally came to an end. One group wanted the region to become a Crown colony directly under British rule. Another group advocated a self-governing entity. Yet another proposed (with plenty of vocal support south of the border) that it be sold or ceded to the United States.

Gradually people moved north from the United States, at first via the long overland wagon trail from St. Paul and, later, via the steamboat traffic that developed between Minnesota and Fort Garry after 1858. The northern migration increased after the HBC territory was taken over by the Canadian government and Manitoba became the nation's fifth province.

Steamboat travel on the Red and Assiniboine Rivers was a great deal faster than travel by canoe, York boat, or ox-drawn Red River cart, which were the alternatives before 1858. But steamboat travel could have more than its fair share of frustrations and delays.

Most years the rivers had a great deal of water in them in spring and early summer, and some years, the smoke-belching, paddlewheel-threshing ships could fulfill their schedules almost until freeze-up. But there were lean years, when rivers were low and harried captains and crews had to resort to a great variety of strategies to keep their vessels afloat.

Sometimes a skipper would "walk" his ship over shallows, using the tall booms that stood upright from the deck near the brow. Or, he would fasten a stout line to a tree or rock on the riverbank some distance ahead of where shallows had stopped him and, using the ship's steam winch, drag his vessel through the shallows until it reached deeper water.

Sometimes a skipper would get his whole crew into the river to construct a wing dam, which would hold back enough water to get the ship through a tough spot. There are records of several instances when everybody on board, including passengers, got out and pushed.

The combination of men and possessions almost inevitably seems to create a state of competition. In the case of men and ships, the result is almost always a race. There are numerous accounts of boats on the Red River being pitted against each other, with pilots using their finest skills or trickery and the crew stoking the fires and raising boiler pressure to within a hair's breadth of disaster.

There is a story in the 1870s *Manitoba Free Press* of a contest between Norman Kittson's *International* and John Griggs' *Selkirk*. The reporter told it this way:

It wasn't a race, exactly, but they—the *Selkirk* and the *International*—both wanted to get a Beetle ahead of the other. They left here a week ago Monday evening, the *International* having three hours start, which she kept until arrival at Pembina, where a delay caused by the breaking of one of her cam yokes allowed the *Selkirk* to catch up. Both boats left that place together, nose to nose, the *Selkirk* took the lead till she broke a wheel arm, which occasioned a stoppage for repairs, during which the *International* passed her. At Grand Forks, the *International* stopped but the rival boat hadn't time.

Mitchell [*Selkirk*'s captain] placed a crewman on the safety valve and was standing over him with a monkey wrench to see that he kept his place. Both boats tore up the river, stole wood from each other [with] *International* reaching Fisher's Landing in Minnesota an hour and a half ahead, said one, and fifteen minutes ahead according to the *Selkirk* version.

Another report in the *Manitoba Free Press* on 26 September 1876 quotes a letter from a passenger who travelled on the *Minnesota*. He wrote that he was awakened by the sound of the ship's whistle and went on deck to see what was going on.

"A night race was on between the *Minnesota* and the *Manitoba*," he wrote. "The great lights of the two steamers gave a weird appearance to the scene. What a racket: the pilots leaned over their wheelhouses and cracked jokes with each other; and the roosters on deck crowed over each other, and the great chimneys puffed and threw out great clouds of sparks in unison, but we didn't spill any coal oil into the furnace nor break up the cabin furniture to make steam, but we forged ahead and soon left the *Manitoba* far in our wake."

The reference to pouring coal oil on the fire to increase boiler

Excitement Included Murder

The passenger lists on the numerous ships plying the waters of the Red River were a cross section of the continent's population. In one instance such a list contributed to a mystery that has never been solved.

In the early 1870s one of the most important figures on the river was Norman Kittson, who owned and operated several of the steamers. One of his ships, the International, arrived at Fort Garry, unloaded its cargo and passengers, and was being prepared for the return trip south when a purser, who had been checking over the cabins, found one door that could not be opened.

Calling out and knocking on the door produced no response. The purser looked at the passenger list and discovered that the cabin had been occupied by a man who had given his name as G. Orton. The captain gave permission for a forced entry.

The window glass was smashed and the smallest member of the crew squirmed into the cabin. He removed a chair that was wedged under the doorknob and reported: "There's a man in the bunk . . . and blood on the pillow . . . Looks as if he's dead."

There was no trace of identification on the body that gave any clue about who the man was. He had boarded the ship at Grand Forks and had kept very much to himself. The only possible lead was a gold Masonic pin in his coat lapel on which was engraved the letter "G."

It was impossible to question any of the other passengers, since they had long disembarked and scattered in various directions. In fact, the officers of the law— few in number and lacking almost all the facilities available to current-day police— were stumped. They weren't even sure that "G. Orton" was the man's real name, since there had been cases of passengers on the run from the law or from creditors or from domestic problems who were virtually untraceable.

Cabin staff remembered that Orton had brought two expensive heavy leather bags on board. He was described as being about forty-five years of age, with a short beard and dressed in clothes that were so ordinary that no one had noticed them.

Examination of the body revealed that Orton had been hit hard from behind and his throat had been cut, the knife slicing through his neck artery, which resulted in splashes of blood on the cabin walls.

As Theodore Barris wrote in his book Fire Canoe: "Fingerprint files did not exist, there was only limited wire communication, and the absence of photographic aids left the authorities empty-handed. If the murderer had calculated the attack, he chose the perfect victim and the perfect time aboard the perfect vehicle. And with little effort, the killer left the International and was swallowed up by a veil of frontier anonymity."

pressure needs no explanation. Perhaps other Red River boat races had involved the use of cabin furniture to avoid stopping for wood when boiler fires were burning more than the usual amount of fuel. However, it is certainly reminiscent of stories about great riverboat races on the Mississippi, where captains desperate for a win burned all movable, or removable, wood onboard.

Even without a race, travel on the Red River was no idyllic voyage. When Canada's first Governor General, Lord Dufferin, made his first visit to Manitoba in 1877, he was accompanied by his wife aboard the *Minnesota*, who wrote of her experience:

> We go from one bank to the other, crushing and crashing against the trees which grow down to the waterside; I had just written this when I gave a shriek as I saw my ink-bottle on the point of being swept overboard by an intrusive tree. The consequence of this curious navigation is that we never really go on for more than three minutes at a time . . . Our sternwheel is very often ashore, and our captain and pilot must require the patience of saints . . .

> Slowly we turned a point and saw another boat approaching us. It looked beautiful in the dark, with two great bull's-eyes [lanterns] green and red lamps and other lights on the deck, creeping towards us; we stopped and backed into the shore that it might pass us. It came close and fired off a cannon and we saw on the deck [of the *Manitoba*] a large transparency with "Welcome Lord Dufferin" on it, and two girls dressed in white with flags in their hands; then a voice sang "Canada, Sweet Canada," and many more voices joined the chorus, and they sang "God Save the King" and "Rule Britannia," and cheered for the Governor-General as they began to move slowly away disappearing into the darkness.

Lord Dufferin and his wife went on to Winnipeg and then boarded the Hudson's Bay Company ship *Colville* for a cruise on Lake Winnipeg. When the viceregal party reboarded the *Minnesota*, their send-off was accompanied by much cheering, shouting, and waving of flags and, according to Lady Dufferin's account, a Member of Parliament "quite overcome by the grief of parting with us, almost fell into the water because he continued his parting speech until the gangway was removed."

Only a few months later Captain Griggs piloted his ship *Selkirk* to a landing stage on the east bank of the Red River, where his cargo was transferred from the barges that had been carrying it. That cargo was the first steam locomotive in western Canada, later named *Countess of Dufferin*. One wonders if Griggs was aware of the significance of his cargo, that it would herald the end of a way of life for the many who plied their trade on the waters of the Red River.

Vote Early, Vote Often

Chaos reigns in the press room of the Manitoban
after election riots in 1872.

ARCHIVES OF MANITOBA (N5827)

Winnipeg came into being during a tempestuous period in Manitoba's development. In fact the city's birth might well have been the only occasion in Canadian history in which a public official was actually tarred for his views.

Manitoba became a province in 1870, and the settlement at the river junction was the logical site for the capital. But, according to the records, Winnipeg's population in 1870 only numbered one hundred. However, by 1874, that number had grown to five thousand, and it was, in the minds of leading citizens, high time for incorporation.

In 1873 a group of prominent men called a meeting at which a proposed legislative bill that would incorporate the city was adopted. After the bill got into the legislature, however, it was so drastically altered that its original supporters withdrew their backing. Many in Winnipeg believed that Donald A. Smith, then a member of the provincial house and a fast-rising official of the Hudson's Bay Company, had been instrumental in having the changes made. It is easy to see why.

The Hudson's Bay Company and one or two other large property owners knew that if Winnipeg became an organized municipality, it would need to generate revenue, and the main source of such revenue would be from property taxes. They, as major landholders in the area, would be hit hardest. As a result of the proposed bill and the changes made to it, there were heated arguments culminating in an episode that seems almost unbelievable today.

The speaker of the legislature, Dr. C. J. Bird, aroused the wrath of someone during the debate on incorporation. Who this person was has never been established, but the fact remains that Bird was called out one snowy evening, ostensibly to see a sick patient. He arrived at an isolated spot on the edge of town and there was set upon by unknown persons who poured a considerable quantity of hot tar over him. Whether or not the miscreants intended to add feathers to the tar isn't known. Bird managed to escape and sought help.

When a large mob gathered at the legislative building to protest the amendments to their act, Bird just didn't feel up to facing them and sent out his deputy, Dr. J. O'Donnell, who urged the crowd to depart and come back with a new bill.

This was done, but when the new bill was presented before the legislative assembly, the people of Winnipeg weren't taking any chances. They crowded right into the chamber and stayed there until the bill was passed.

And so Winnipeg became a city on 1 January 1874.

Nominations for mayor and council had been held a few days earlier on 29 December 1873, and the first civic election was held on 5 January 1874. There was no secret ballot in those days, nor did every adult resident of the city have a vote. There were a mere 388 qualified electors on the voters list, and each of these had to go into the polling station, announce his name, and state his choice between the candidates for office.

When the results were tallied, they showed that, despite there being only 388 electors, 562 votes had been cast—383 for Francis E. Cornish and 179 for his opponent, W. F. Luxton. Cornish was a lawyer from Ontario who had played a major role in the incorporation campaign, and Luxton was a newspaperman.

According to city hall records, it was somehow established that Cornish's total included 175 "illegal repeaters," while Luxton's tally included only five over-enthusiastic supporters. It was a case of the old adage "vote early and vote often" put into practice. There is no satisfactory account available of the creative arithmetic used to produce the decision by election officials that Cornish had a majority of eighty-eight.

Cornish was sworn in as mayor, and city council's first act was the appointment of Colin F. Strang as mayor's auditor. Members of the council were known as aldermen in those days, and one of the first in that council was J. H. Ashdown, whose hardware empire later grew across western Canada.

The new city's first chief of police was John S. Ingram, who was appointed on 19 February 1874, in good time to deal with the city's first recorded burglary on 5 June.

The fire department of the new city got its first modern, steam-powered pumper on 28 November 1874 and, on 12 January 1875 it was used to douse a restaurant fire, having responded to the alarm within three-and-a-half minutes.

In those days, the mayor sat in court as the city's chief magistrate. Mayor Cornish's unconventional style was demonstrated when he was himself charged with a breach of a municipal bylaw. Appearing before himself, he fined himself five dollars, and then remitted the fine on account of previous good behaviour.

Cornish served one term and was succeeded by William Nassau Kennedy, who later led the Manitoba contingent on the ill-fated Nile expedition of 1883 (see "Voyageurs on the Nile," page 150).

Cornish remained active in local politics. During the 1876 election he and some friends showed their concern about the results of the vote in one ward. In fact, Cornish, Alderman W. B. Thibodeau, and two news-papermen, J. R. Cameron and W. G. Elliott, forced their way into the home of the returning officer and, after a scuffle, made off with the poll book. Such well-known figures as these were quickly apprehended. Cornish and Thibodeau were fined twenty dollars each and the news-papermen "left the country, never to return," as Fred Lucas put it in his *Historical Diary of Winnipeg*.

Winnipeg's early councils were concerned with a number of matters that are no longer of any consequence, but some of their problems have their modern counterparts. Within ten years of incorporation, city council was trying to cope with the pervasive mud by paving a stretch of Main Street with wood blocks and tar. Store closing hours, dance halls, and traffic were matters of increasing interest, and in February 1890, Mayor Alfred Pearson proposed that city council permit women who were property owners to be candidates for office. The proposal was swiftly voted down.

All these widely varied concerns and problems made Winnipeg an interesting city in those days and, doubtless, a difficult one for the elected municipal representatives to govern. But the city had its advantages, too. Dr. George Grant, principal of Queen's University, visited Winnipeg in 1872 and again in 1881. Comparing these two visits, he wrote: "The first thing that strikes us is that incongruous blending of the new and the old, of barbarism jostling against civilization, that distinguishes every corner of Winnipeg and every phase of its life."

One of the
Wickedest Cities

*Main Street, Winnipeg, in 1902 shows the
multiplicity of bars and liquor outlets.*

ARCHIVES OF MANITOBA (N7968)

When Winnipeg became a city in 1874, many believed it was destined to become the Chicago of the North, a transportation hub, a centre of commerce, and a leader in all things leading to prosperity.

Personalities inevitably played a big part in municipal elections, and no civic election campaign was complete without some charges being voiced and aspersions cast. Generally speaking, however, the members of city council presented a more or less united front with the business and commercial elite of Winnipeg when any outsider cast doubts on the city's current condition or on its future. So, in 1909 when articles began to appear in eastern newspapers about vice and corruption in Winnipeg, the local business community and city council both expressed indignation and anger at this assault on their fair city and their way of doing things.

The *Toronto Globe* started the ball rolling with an article headlined, "Social Evil Runs Riot in Winnipeg, Vice District Growing, Every Den an Illicit Liquor Dive." Other papers ran stories about graft in the municipal government and cast serious doubts on the enforcement of the law in Winnipeg.

The *Globe* article arose out of an interview with a Presbyterian minister, Reverend Dr. J. G. Shearer. Three years earlier Shearer had been one of the prime movers in getting the federal parliament to pass the Lord's Day Act, which placed numerous restrictions on what activities were legal on Sundays. The article described Winnipeg as being "the rottenest city in Canada" and also as the "wickedest city" in the country, charges which produced a strong reaction in the city. The leaders of Winnipeg were not only offended but also concerned by what they saw as serious deterrents to attracting immigrants and investors. Of course, there had always been complaints about "wickedness" in Winnipeg.

Civic concern began as far back as 1874 when the city received a petition from a taxpayer demanding the city remove what were referred to as "houses of ill fame." A campaign against prostitution began in 1883 led by the Winnipeg Ministerial Association, resulting in the adoption by the city and the police of a "segregation" policy. This meant that brothels were confined to one small area of the city. Most of the "houses of ill fame" had been located west of Sherbrooke Street and north of Queen Street, as Portage Avenue was then called. The new policy shifted them all to a small portion of Point Douglas. The women were forbidden to solicit on the street and, if they wished to move about the city, could only do so in closed vehicles.

In *Winnipeg: An Illustrated History*, Alan Artibise notes that: "The prostitutes were also told that it was to their benefit to carry on a quiet business for there was no telling what might happen if the clergy got wind of this arrangement." Artibise then quotes the *Winnipeg Times* of 3 April 1883, which opined editorially that, "Clergymen are not the most intelligent men, nor do they reason the best."

The first decade of the twentieth century was one of amazing growth as Winnipeg became the centre through which almost all the trade to and from the west flowed via the railroad. Construction trades boomed and there was a steady flow of incomers. Some of the newcomers intended to take up land, while others were the inevitable drifters and grifters who were attracted to centres where there were prospects of easy pickings. The increase in wealth and population also caused an increase in the number of prostitutes, who soon became too numerous for the area to which they were restricted. They occupied more than one hundred brothels.

By 1910 there was a strong reform movement in Winnipeg that was part of a movement sweeping the continent. A Moral and Social Reform League was established, led by Dr. Shearer. This organization condemned the segregation policy, which wasn't working, and called for "better social and moral conditions." It drew support not only from most churches but also from the Anti-Saloon League and the Winnipeg Trades and Labour Council, which represented the unions then gaining strength in the city.

The Moral Reform League's campaign was underway as municipal politicians were beginning to get ready for the annual election. E. D. Martin was put forward as the mayoral candidate of the group opposed to the policy of segregating prostitutes, and faced a third-term bid by the sitting mayor, Sanford Evans, who owned a daily paper called the *Winnipeg Telegram*.

It was a vicious campaign, with Evans's supporters charging that Martin was the voice of foreign agitators and Martin responding by saying that "it is not the good name of the city that is on trial at this election [but] the action of men who, in defiance of the law, set up conditions which inevitably reflect upon the city's good name."

Evans was re-elected by a majority of almost two thousand votes.

The brothels in Point Douglas continued to operate. There were occasional arrests of prostitutes and warnings given whenever some vocal person or group raised the issue. In *Red Lights on the Prairies*, James Gray wrote that, in spite of sporadic clean-up campaigns, the brothels in Point Douglas and across the river in what is now East Kildonan were in business without too much interference for close to thirty years, until amateur competition reduced demand for their services.

Although most of the "ladies of easy virtue," as they were called, probably resorted to prostitution as the only way they knew to support themselves, there appeared to be little concern for their well-being. It was generally assumed that they were prostitutes by choice and happy with that choice. More recently, with the involvement of organized crime and drugs, the prostitution industry has lost what tawdry glamour it may have once had. Even so, there is seldom a public outcry against it as it is out of sight for most people. But it is a concern for those living in areas where the sex, and accompanying drug, trade is openly conducted and for those working to assist women trapped on the streets by poverty or addiction.

As no amount of policing ever seems to remove, or reduce, prostitution, there have been occasional calls for the return of the brothels to Winnipeg; this time organized, government-controlled, legal brothels. While most people doubt that this will ever happen, one cannot be so sure. After all, look at what has happened over a few years to what was once illegal gambling.

Walking Out on Thin Ice

*Stephen "Steve" Juba (on the right,) Winnipeg's
longest serving mayor, is seen here with
John McDiarmid and Lewis Foote.*

A man of wide experience once said: "A person who is mayor of a city must be like someone who goes out on that thin, rubbery ice that forms over a river or lake after the first heavy freeze: constantly alert, quick on the feet and, if he doesn't want to get into deep water, always sure of a way back to solid ground." It sounds cynical, perhaps, but it is not without a considerable amount of truth.

The office of mayor gets its name from the Latin word major, meaning greater, and it was adopted as the title for the leader of town government to indicate that he was more powerful, either in prestige or in actual administrative clout, than the other councillors.

Dozens of men—and one woman—have held the position of mayor in the years since Winnipeg became an incorporated city. Since the mayor's term of office was only one year at a time from 1874 to 1940, there was considerable turnover during the first half-century of Winnipeg's history. During this period thirteen mayors enjoyed only one year in office, some of them being defeated when they tried for a second term. The city's first mayor, Francis Evans Cornish, was among those one-termers.

The second mayor, William Nassau Kennedy, was an officer in the militia. He led the Manitoba contingent that accompanied General Garnet Wolseley on an unsuccessful attempt to rescue General Charles Gordon from Khartoum in the Anglo-Egyptian Sudan. On his way home, Kennedy died in England from an illness contracted during the expedition.

There were one or two mayors who kept coming back after varying intervals out of office, such as Alexander Logan who held office in 1879 and 1880, came back in 1882, and held the position again in 1884.

Alfred Pearson, who held office in 1890 and 1891, is remembered for his unsuccessful efforts to persuade city council to allow female property owners to qualify as candidates for council. Another mayor, whose name became almost a household word in western Canada as the builder of a retail hardware empire, was James Henry Ashdown, who held the city's top post during 1907 and 1908.

One of the more interesting personalities in Winnipeg's municipal life was Richard Deans Waugh. Mayor in 1912 and again in 1915 and 1916, Waugh became well known not only in Winnipeg but also internationally. He is remembered by the name of the townsite where the Greater Winnipeg Water District pipeline starts to take water from Shoal Lake for the use of Winnipeggers.

A great believer in the beneficial effects of gardening, Waugh set up and founded what used to be known as the Waugh Shield Garden Competition for schoolchildren. Children of various ages were encouraged by their schools to enter, and each received a variety of seeds and detailed instructions on the layout of their garden plots. Volunteers with horticultural knowledge were enlisted to make periodic inspections of the Waugh gardens and to offer advice. At the end of the summer, the gardens were assessed and marked, and the school with the highest score earned by its students was awarded temporary possession of the Waugh Shield, with a suitably inscribed plate added to the trophy.

After the First World War, Waugh entered the world stage when he was appointed Canada's representative on the international commission struck by the League of Nations to govern the Saarland province of Germany.

The mayoralty election of 1916 was contested by two city business leaders, David J. Dyson and Frederick Harvey Davidson. Dyson was head of the Dyson Pickle Company, a prominent enterprise in Winnipeg at the time.

When the votes were counted on election night, Dyson was declared the winner with a count of 5,009 to 4,991. Davidson claimed the victory, however, charging that a number of ballots marked for him had been entered in the books—by error or not—as Dyson's. The *Winnipeg Free Press* of 5 January 1917, right after Dyson had been sworn in, ran a story with the headline, "Who is Mayor of Winnipeg?"

Judge H. Myers held a judicial recount on 6 January that resulted in a count of 5,019 for Davidson and 4,999 for Dyson, who was unseated. Davidson was sworn in, but not without protests from Dyson, who charged a number of irregularities had taken place and called for a new election. In his petition, he referred to "the pretended election of Davidson," adding the latter "was not necessarily qualified under the act," and claimed that numerous impersonations had taken place at the polls.

A city lawyer interested in the case was quoted as saying, "We know

The Reign of Stephen Juba

Mayor Stephen Juba was a departure from tradition. For the first time in Winnipeg's history, city council would be led by a representative of the city's ethnic population. Juba was of Ukrainian origin. He had served a term as a member of the legislature and was, in fact, still an MLA when he was first elected as mayor.

While an MLA Juba had gained a good deal of publicity by his tireless campaign to have provincial liquor laws amended. When this happened, Juba's name was firmly fixed in the public mind as that of the man who had inspired the changes and, from 1956 until 1977, he was a shoo-in at every election.

Juba's name is associated with many major events in the city's history. He lobbied for and won the 1967 Pan American Games for Winnipeg, which spawned construction of the Pan-Am Pool, the Velodrome, and the University Stadium.

He was noted for his grand but sometimes unclear ideas for the city. The most-often cited of these was his dream of setting up a monorail rapid transit system to link all parts of the city with a fast and efficient way of moving people.

In 1960 the provincial government began an experiment in municipal administration modelled after Toronto's experience of a few years earlier, calling it the Metropolitan Corporation of Greater Winnipeg. This metropolitan council was to have authority over the various services that affected all of the thirteen cities, towns, and municipalities centred on the forks of the Red and Assiniboine Rivers —services such as transit, water, and traffic control.

The idea of a level of municipal government that seemed to be above that of the city did not sit well with Steve Juba, and he was not amused by facetious references to the chairman of the metropolitan council, R. G. H. (Dick) Bonnycastle, as the "Supermayor." The ten years of Metro's existence were years of a running feud between Juba and the metropolitan council chairman.

It was, therefore, a great relief to Mayor Juba—and to many others— when the province amalgamated all the municipal governments into one big city. Juba was elected easily in the first vote held by the new civic authority and continued in office for seven more years before his retirement in 1977. He died in 1993 at the age of seventy-eight.

that in one ballot box, there were 56 bogus ballots." Dyson's claims were set aside, however, although he gave up with a strong statement urging that opportunities for plural or bogus balloting be done away with.

Charles Gray, mayor in 1919–20, presided over city council during the momentous days of the Winnipeg General Strike and was the official who read the Riot Act from the steps of the old City Hall on Main Street. This act authorized the use of force against demonstrators who refused to disperse. As a result of the act's authorization, the Royal North-West Mounted Police charged the crowd. There was gunfire and two men died—one was an innocent onlooker.

Edward Parnell was mayor from 1921 until 9 June 1922 when he died. He was succeeded by Frank O. Fowler, who won a by-election on 30 June. His six-month term was the shortest of any Winnipeg mayor. He was defeated by the city's first Labour Party representative, Seymour Farmer. Farmer won a second term in 1924.

The era of long terms in office began in 1925 with Lieutenant Colonel Ralph Humphreys Webb. Webb's First World War service ended when he was so badly wounded in one leg that he had to amputate the shattered limb himself. He was, at the time of his election, manager of the Marlborough Hotel (formerly the Olympia).

Given to off-the-cuff comments in a brusque, no-nonsense manner, Webb had a special dislike for radicals of any sort. All of them were, in his view, lumped together under the generic heading of Communists. He was quoted as saying that radical troublemakers, such as those who, he claimed, had brought about the Winnipeg General Strike of 1919, should be "thrown into the Red River."

Webb's artificial leg was somewhat noisy, and its proud owner made good use of it. He could always be heard approaching by the "click, squeak, thump" that sounded loud and clear as he took each step.

After his first three terms (1925–27), Webb was replaced by another military man, Lieutenant Colonel Dan McLean, but in 1930 Webb returned and held the mayoralty for five more years until the end of 1934.

Winnipeg's second Labour mayor, John Queen, was also a member of the legislature, a double duty that was legal at the time. With the exception of 1937, Queen was mayor until the end of 1942. From 1942 to 1971, the mayor's term was two years, after which it was extended to three years.

Queen was a natural on the platform, able to get a crowd laughing even if they didn't agree with what he said. He was an able negotiator and a master at making platitudes sound like profound wisdom. Queen was defeated by Garnet Coulter, who held the position for an unprecedented twelve years.

During Coulter's term many changes occurred in the city. During the war, resources that might have been used to maintain a balanced supply of homes for Winnipeg's increased population were instead funnelled into the war effort. Coulter had to find the resources to house the servicemen and women who came home after the war.

The longest mayoralty term of all was that of Stephen Juba, who ran the score up to twenty-one uninterrupted years of service, during which he was credited with bringing the Pan American Games to the city for the first time, presiding over vast changes to Winnipeg's face, and conducting a running battle with the short-lived Metropolitan Corporation of Greater Winnipeg (see sidebar, "The Reign of Stephen Juba").

After Juba finally left the scene in 1977, there was an immediate scramble for the vacant position. This was won by Robert Steen, who was destined to die in office early in 1979. His successor, William Norrie, won the position in a by-election on 30 June 1979. Norrie also joined the ranks of Winnipeg's longest-serving mayors, holding fast to the office until 1992 when he was succeeded by Winnipeg's first female mayor, Susan A. Thompson. She served until 1998 when Glen Murray was elected.

A Manitoba
Ghost Town

The 10 August 1880 issue of the Nelsonville
Manitoba Mountaineer.

The words "ghost town" usually bring to mind abandoned wooden buildings slowly falling apart in a dusty, windy, desert town once populated by plodding prospectors, pack-laden burros, hard-faced gunslingers, solemn saloon keepers, dance hall girls with hearts of gold, a drunken and/or devoted doctor, a hapless sheriff, and sundry (and always timid) citizens. There may have been a few such towns, but they are largely the figments of Hollywood imaginations.

We may find it hard to apply the term "ghost town" to any place in Manitoba. But many small towns or villages, which once were community centres with populations of up to a thousand, are now no more than one or two weather-greyed and decaying buildings. Some have completely disappeared.

For instance, who has ever heard of Nelsonville, Manitoba?

Nelsonville, which enjoyed less than a dozen years of prosperous life, was located about 125 kilometres (78 mi.) southwest of Winnipeg. Its story began in 1877 when the transcontinental CPR rail line was still no more than a dream, although work had begun on a railway line from Winnipeg to Pembina on the American border. Adam Nelson, an Ontario farmer, decided to come west and bought land where the future town would be located. When he arrived with his family, he found his property was not open land as he had expected, but heavily treed.

Nelson turned his unwelcome surprise into an asset by deciding that if he couldn't farm without a lot of effort, he could produce lumber, for which there was a growing demand in the southern part of the province. He obtained equipment for both a sawmill and a gristmill and, in November 1877, freighted it in. Thus, the nucleus of Nelsonville was created.

By 1880 a thriving community had developed as a result of Nelson's ingenuity. Henry J. Pugh in his *Early Settlement of Pembina Mountain District* wrote: "There were three general stores, two hotels, two private banks, two hardware stores, a furniture store, bakery, grocery and liquor store, real estate offices, three law offices, three doctors, a harness shop, a woodworking shop, a jewellery store, a drug store, two blacksmith's shops, two large livery and feed barns, and all the enterprises and

Moving the Manitoba Mountaineer

What does the editor of a weekly newspaper do when the citizens of the town he serves decide to move—move the whole town that is, including buildings? He joins them, of course.

In 1880 the Manitoba Mountaineer *started publication in the bustling settlement of Nelsonville (later known simply as Nelson) under the auspices of owner/editor J. H. Galbraith.*

While the town was celebrating the third anniversary of its incorporation, the Canadian Pacific Railway, which had earlier bought out the Manitoba Colonization Railroad that was intended to pass through Nelsonville, announced that its Pembina branch would be routed through Plum Coulee and westward to Pilot Mound, bypassing Nelsonville by several miles. As a result, the citizens of Nelsonville decided to move—the whole town.

For the next year or so, the roads and trails between the dying town and the new town, which was to become Morden, were well travelled as the town relocated. Galbraith loaded up his type, press, and other equipment, and joined the steady stream trekking to a new townsite in 1884. On 31 October 1884 he produced the first issue of the Manitoba News *from his new office in Morden.*

"We have been laboring [sic] under serious difficulties in getting out our first issue of the Manitoba News," *he wrote. "The weather is inclement and our building is far from complete; our printing material has all to be removed from* Nelson during the current week and is yet in rank disorder; our printers are exhausted with overwork and the unaccustomed exertion consequent on moving heavy printing presses; and, lastly, we are ourselves annoyed and worried out of all semblance of equanimity. But we love to fulfill our agreements and had the difficulties been twice as great, yet would the Manitoba News *have commenced publication on or before the first of November."*

Galbraith shut down the News *in March 1887 and moved to British Columbia. Two new papers, each with political connections, succeeded the* News. *However, as many ambitious publishers later discovered, towns the size of Morden could not support two weeklies, and the new papers, the* Monitor *and the* Herald, *were more or less amalgamated in 1897. Galbraith returned to edit the new paper, called the* Morden Chronicle.

For almost four years Galbraith wrote colourful, pointed, and well-informed articles on a variety of subjects relating to the community's well-being. But in 1898, a new paper, the Morden Empire, *made its appearance and, to quote A. M. Pratt (in* The Story of Manitoba's Weekly Newspapers), *"under changing editorship, caused considerable embarrassment" to the veteran editor of the* Chronicle. *In 1901 Galbraith again retired to British Columbia, having written himself into the story of Manitoba's newspapers as one who "slung a mean pen."*

conveniences that civilized beings required." But no railway.

A weekly newspaper named the *Manitoba Mountaineer* published its first issue in Nelsonville on 8 September 1880 under the editorship of J. H. Galbraith (see sidebar, "Moving the *Manitoba Mountaineer*").

Five years after Adam Nelson took possession of his land, the settlement was incorporated as the Town of Nelsonville (some years later, the town lost the "-ville" and became known as just Nelson). Farms were being established in the district and producing crops for sale, but everything for shipment had to be hauled by wagon to Emerson, a distance of about 113 kilometres (70 mi.). The real estate boom in Winnipeg had spread to Nelson where, according to Mulligan and Ryder, speculators offered one thousand dollars per lot in the new town. But there was still no railway.

There had been much talk and some forecasts that a Pembina branch of the CPR would be built west of the line between Winnipeg and the United States, but the Manitoba Colonization Railway, which was to have constructed this route, was bought out by the CPR.

Under the headline "Gobbling of the Manitoba South-Western by the CPR," Galbraith wrote: "This iniquity was consummated last fall. Winter had come and gone but not a single additional mile has been constructed. [CPR General Manager] Van Horne . . . has been good enough to say that the south-western road will be built as soon as money can be provided, but in the meantime who will provide bread for the hungry mouths or clothes to cover the nakedness of the shivering little ones?"

The editorial quoted Van Horne as saying that: "There is no possibility of our being able to extend either the Manitoba South-Western or the Pembina Branch this season for want of funds; but if the crop turns out as well as it promises, and if the people will give us half a chance we will be able to commence work on one of our branch lines early next spring."

The announced route for the southwestern line was through Treherne, Holland, and Glenboro—too far north for Nelson, but the people of the town still had hopes for the Pembina line going through their settlement.

The final announcement detailing the Pembina branch route was a fatal blow to Nelson. The CPR laid out its line through Plum Coulee and due west to Pilot Mound, just over 6 kilometres (4 mi.) north of Nelson. The town's nearest station on the new railway branch would be a converted boxcar located on the farm of Alvey Morden.

So on the basis of the old adage, "If you can't lick 'em, join 'em," the people of Nelson set about moving themselves, and their town, the six kilometres. The population of Nelson soon made up the major part of Morden.

Everything moved. Henry Pugh wrote: "The exodus started in 1884 and by 1885 was in full swing so that daily was [a] common sight to see a number of buildings on trucks or skids moving steadily to the new Eldorado—the town of Morden."

So Nelson—a.k.a. Nelsonville—disappeared to become, in fact, the ghost of a ghost town, since the buildings have all gone. According to Mulligan and Ryder, "a cairn is all that remains of a once bustling and optimistic prairie community."

Voyageurs on the Nile

*The grave and gravestone of Boatman Adam
Cochrane notes his involvement in the Egyptian
Expeditionary Force 1884–85.*

DON AIKEN

There is a little stone church on the east bank of the Red River, a few miles below Selkirk. It is a quiet, rather lonely place, although in recent years it has been refurbished and the grounds, including the attached graveyard, have been given much better care than they had received for many years.

St. Peter's Church, or St. Peter's Dynevor as it is better known, stands on the site of the first Indian mission in western Canada, which was founded in 1833. The present structure was built in 1854 and is one of the oldest stone churches in the west.

Around the church, there are graves old and new. The names and dates help visitors to trace something of the history of the area and of the families who have been members of this Anglican parish for more than a century and a half. In this peaceful rural setting, the inscriptions on two gravestones transport the visitor far from the relatively small Red River to one of the world's mightiest streams—the Nile.

How could there be a link between the north African river of ancient history, on whose waters the pharaohs of Egypt rode in splendour thousands of years ago, and the Red River of fur trade fame, known to Europeans for only 250 years or so?

The wording on the stones is plain:

BOATMAN ADAM COCHRANE
1849–1935
Egyptian Expeditionary Force 1884–5

BOATMAN ALEXANDER COCHRANE
1845–1927
Egyptian Expeditionary Force 1884–5

Who were the Cochranes? How did they get to Egypt? And why?

Regarding who they were, the records are scanty. Although they were presumably members of the parish, the registers in the keeping of the Diocese of Rupert's Land note only their deaths and burials and give no clue about their place of birth or details of their families. One may extrapolate, however, that they worked on the river, handling the York boats and other vessels of the time used mainly in freighting and the fur trade.

How and why they went to Egypt is another matter, for the expedition in which they took part is well chronicled.

In the early 1880s a devout Muslim leader rose in the Sudan, regarded at the time as being part of Egypt. He was acclaimed as the *Mahdi,* a messiah and long-awaited leader who would guide the oppressed to freedom under religious rule. The Egyptian government's armies suffered a number of defeats at the hands of the *Mahdi's* forces and asked the British to lend them a general who could withstand, and perhaps turn back, the advance of the Mahdists. General Charles Gordon was chosen and was sent to the Sudanese capital of Khartoum, where he was very soon besieged by the massive armies of the Muslim leader.

Another general, Lord Garnet Wolseley, was selected to lead an expeditionary force to relieve Khartoum and rescue Gordon. Wolseley had served in Canada, and one of his principal duties here had been to lead the small army sent from eastern Canada to put down the Red River Rebellion of 1869–70. Wolseley had been greatly impressed by the skill of Canadian boatmen in navigating the swift-flowing and broken waters of Canada's rivers. He was convinced that men who could deal with Canadian rapids could also deal with the Nile's six great cataracts through which his expedition would have to battle its way to reach Khartoum.

Wolseley decided that three to four hundred Canadian boatmen would be just the thing he needed to get his army up the great river. He asked Governor General Lord Lansdowne for help in recruiting what Wolseley called "good voyageurs from Caughnawaga, Saint Regis, and Manitoba." Prime Minister Sir John A. Macdonald didn't oppose the idea, but he made it clear that the boatmen were to be the responsibility of the British, not the Canadian, government.

Initially the pay offered was forty dollars a month, plus clothing suitable for the work and the climate. When the boatmen finally were assembled in Montreal to board the chartered liner *Ocean King*, they numbered 386, of whom 92 were from Manitoba. Half of the whole group was literate, and about a hundred were Indian or Métis.

In addition, a number of bewhiskered riverboat captains, four of them from Manitoba, were hired to act as steersmen of the steamers Wolseley planned to use on the Nile. The Manitoba group included:

William Robinson, J. Weber, R. A. Russell, and John S. Seeger. Only Robinson was a Canadian, the others were American citizens who had commanded steamers on the Red River and Lake Winnipeg.

The Manitoba contingent weren't all boatmen by any means. Lieutenant Colonel William Nassau Kennedy, Winnipeg's second mayor and devoted militia officer, went along, too, as did three of his fellow officers.

The effort to rescue Gordon almost succeeded. Just two days before Wolseley's army came in sight of Khartoum, the city fell to the Mahdists and Gordon was killed. The relief expedition had to retreat downstream to Egypt.

Sixteen of the Canadian boatmen died, either drowning, or struck down by disease or accident. The great majority of them started for home early in 1885, under the leadership of Kennedy. However, the boatmen had to return to Canada without him. It was discovered that Kennedy had contracted smallpox in Egypt and he died in London.

As for Adam and Alexander Cochrane of St. Peter's: after they returned home their story fades into the obscurity of history. They probably went back to work on the more familiar waters of the Red River, and tales of their experiences must surely have entertained their friends for many years.

One Paddlewheel
Ticket to Brandon,
Please

The steamboat Alberta *took employees of the Hudson's Bay
Company up the Red River for their annual picnic.*

ARCHIVES OF MANITOBA (N3706)

The steamboat industry on the Red and Assiniboine Rivers started in 1859 when Anson Northup, an old Mississippi River hand, piloted a stubby little steamer that bore his name, from Lafayette, Minnesota, to Upper Fort Garry. His arrival on 10 June that year was cause for great celebration—and some deep thinking on the part of the all-powerful Hudson's Bay Company.

Until the *Northup*'s hoarse whistle awoke the settlement at the river forks, astonishing the Natives and drawing cheers from the settlers, the HBC had enjoyed a monopoly on trade with the outside world. Almost everything the Red River Settlement and many of the western fur trade forts needed came through the HBC establishments on Hudson Bay.

Northrup's arrival represented competition with a vengeance. Not only were American entrepreneurs likely to expand this new trade channel, but the HBC began to fear what was the start of an expansionist mood in the United States, which gave rise to the phrase "manifest destiny" to describe the belief shared by some Americans that they were intended to rule the entire continent. Bishop Alexandre Taché of St. Boniface wrote: "A new era for our country was being inaugurated. Each turn of the engine appeared to bring us nearer by so much to the civilized world."

The HBC tried boycotting goods brought in by steamboat, and it was only a matter of months before the boycott forced Northup to sell his ship—for eight thousand dollars—to a firm called J. C. Burbank and Company. The *Northup* was renamed *Pioneer* and went to work for her new owners, who had the Hudson's Bay Company as a silent partner.

From spring breakup until fall freeze-up, *Pioneer* threshed its way north and south on the Red River, but its career was cut short in 1862 when it was caught by the ice at Cook's Creek and was crushed. The demise of *Pioneer* marked the start of an eight-year gap in river traffic because the American Civil War was taking up all that country's energy, and, in addition, a widespread and violent uprising of the Sioux nations in Minnesota made any sort of travel south unsafe.

When steamboating resumed in 1870, it was marked by the arrival of *International*, built in Minnesota by J. C. Davis and sold to the Burbank

Company, still bankrolled by the HBC. About 41 metres (135 ft.) long and with a large freight and passenger capacity, *International* arrived at Red River in the middle of one of the area's greatest political upheavals—the Red River Rebellion. Aboard *International* was Captain William F. Butler of the Canadian army. Butler's mission was to meet with Métis leader, Louis Riel.

Riel knew Butler was coming and intended to give him a less-than-friendly reception, but Butler slipped ashore and made his way to Lower Fort Garry. Once there he was able to arrange a meeting with Riel at which he warned the Métis leader of the twelve-hundred-man force being led west by Colonel Garnet Wolseley. After, Riel departed for the United States and the Red River Rebellion ended.

From then until the arrival of the transcontinental railway in 1885, riverboats had the transportation business all to themselves. At the height of the river-shipping boom, there were daily return trips to Portage la Prairie, twice weekly runs to Brandon, daily departures from and to the United States, and, in good years when the water was high, ships ventured as far as Fort Ellice in what is now Saskatchewan. In addition, shipping ran from Winnipeg and Selkirk down to Lake Winnipeg and, later, up the Saskatchewan River by way of Grand Rapids.

We are often told that our history is dull, that we have no outstanding figures to match those of the United States. The many Canadians who appear to believe this haven't learned about aspects of this country's past, including the history of western steamboating.

There are tragedy and comedy, heroics and humour to be found in the wild and sometimes cutthroat battle for supremacy in the river trade. It has been written about, but the stories, somehow, were never too widely circulated. Nothing is left in visible form of those tumultuous days, except for two ships now beached for good.

Fortunately, some people with an eye for history and an appreciation of the lessons of the past set up the Marine Museum of Manitoba at Selkirk (see sidebar, "Saved from the Slough"). There, the SS *Keenora* and the *Bradbury* sit up on the riverbank, largely restored and refurbished, and open to visitors who want a glimpse of the old ways of travelling.

Keenora was launched on Lake of the Woods in 1898. In 1918 a Winnipeg syndicate bought her, had her cut in two, and hauled the halves to Winnipeg by rail. She was stretched to 48.8 metres (160 ft.), cabins and a promenade deck were added, and she went into the cruise trade. In 1923

Saved from the Slough

The middle of the North American continent seems an unlikely place for a tradition of marine activity to thrive, but from 1859 until the 1980s, the Red and the Assiniboine Rivers and Lake Winnipeg carried a great variety of steam-driven, and later diesel-powered, craft of every size and shape. It's only fitting that some tribute be paid to Manitoba's unusual marine heritage. The Marine Museum of Manitoba at Selkirk is a collection of old ships and machinery as well as smaller items relating to the great days of steamboating in Manitoba.

Located at the entrance to Selkirk Park on the banks of the Red River, the museum was incorporated in 1972. The largest vessel in the collection is the MS Keenora (formerly SS for steamship), which travelled the Red River and Lake Winnipeg from 1918 to 1967. When she was tied up in "the slough" at Selkirk in 1967, there was a rumour that interested people in Kenora—where the ship had been rebuilt—wanted to ship her back to her original home. According to Selkirk sources, this was one of the main reasons why the museum was started.

Government grants were sought and other funds were raised by the people of the Selkirk district, who responded generously to the idea of preserving a major feature of their heritage. The museum's first major acquisition, Keenora, was bought for ten thousand dollars.

Photographs, letters, diaries, logbooks, and other documents connected with the Keenora's years of service were gradually collected, as were items of ship's equipment and artifacts of the steamboating era. A base on which to place the ship was constructed.

Another ship included in the collection is the Canadian Government Ship Bradbury. The Selkirk museum board obtained the Bradbury from the Crown Assets Disposal Corporation for the nominal price of thirteen thousand dollars. Thus another piece of Lake Winnipeg history was pulled out of the water, installed on the riverbank, and restored in 1976.

Two other sizable vessels that saw long service on the lake, the Lady Canadian and the Chickama II, are also included in the museum's display. Chickama II was built in 1942 for the Selkirk Navigation Company and served for almost thirty years as a fishery supply vessel. The Lady Canadian was built for Canadian Fish Products in 1944 and was used for a time as a survey vessel.

The two smallest ships in the collection are the Peguis II and the Jackie S. The Peguis II was built in local shipyards in 1955 and saw decades of service as a government tug. The Jackie S. is a traditional Lake Winnipeg fishing vessel.

The museum also boasts a collection of old diving suits and air pumping equipment that were once used in salvage and inspection operations on the lake and the rivers. There are charts of Lake Winnipeg, photographs of many of the vessels that once made these waters busy thoroughfares, letters from travellers who rode on Keenora, and mementos of distinguished visitors.

An appropriate feature at the entrance to the museum is the old lighthouse from Black Bear Island, built in 1898, whose beacon flashes brightly when the museum is open.

Loss of the Alpha

In April 1885 the steamboat Alpha was wrecked near the town of Cypress River—that's Cypress River, Manitoba, about as unlikely a place for a shipwreck as you can imagine.

Alpha was a hardworking ship, hauling freight and passengers out of Winnipeg along the Red–Assiniboine River system before the railway came to western Canada. The boat was owned by a colourful and widely known entrepreneur, Norman W. Kittson, one of the many adventurous characters who battled the adverse conditions of prairie waterways to supply the needs of an expanding region.

There's not much left of the fleet of more than one hundred steamships of all sizes and shapes that brought sternwheel shipping to the west. Most of them were wrecked, sunk, or burned. Of the Alpha, all that remains today is the stern timber, which, embedded in concrete with a small informational plaque, stands at the side of Highway 2 near Cypress River.

Back in the nineteenth century, Manitoba riverboat captains made every effort to get an early start in the year, partly because the season was short and partly because the rivers in those parts have a disconcerting habit of creating sandbars one day where none existed the day before.

So, in April 1885, Alpha set off from Winnipeg with a cargo of freight for Portage la Prairie and Brandon. The Assiniboine River was high with spring runoff and, to save time, the skipper decided to cut across some of the river's many bends. He left the channel and headed over to what is now Spruce Woods Provincial Park. Unfortunately, the method of cutting corners, which had worked for other captains in the past, just didn't work for Alpha. She hit a sandbar and stuck fast.

While the crew was ashore trying to round up manpower to get them off the sandbar, someone with a larcenous turn of mind plundered the cargo and some of the ship's equipment. Alpha never did get off that bank. Every year floodwaters dumped more silt on her hulk, trees grew up around her, and for many years her actual resting place was concealed and forgotten.

Some fifty years after the wreck happened, a change in the river's course carved away all the debris that had hidden Alpha's hull. Over time, the oak timbers were carted away for local use.

she was bought by the Northern Fish Company, for which she hauled mail, food, equipment, and luxuries to settlements that had no other means of transportation on Lake Winnipeg—such as Grand Rapids, Warren Landing, Berens River, and Norway House—and brought back fish.

Keenora converted to diesel in 1960 and, five years later, was finally retired. She was rescued from the fate of many of her predecessors—slow decay in the slough at Selkirk—in 1972, when the Marine Museum was established.

Another ship preserved by the museum, the Bradbury, was launched in 1915 by the federal government as an all-purpose vessel to help the lake shipping trade. She was beautifully finished inside, with oak panelling and quite luxurious furnishings. *Bradbury* was used to maintain the lighthouses and buoys on the lake, and as an icebreaker when occasion demanded. In 1917 she smashed through ice to bring medical assistance to a settlement hard hit by the flu epidemic, and, several years later, she rescued the ss *Grand Rapids*, which was in danger of breaking up on George Island.

The *Lord Selkirk II*, launched in 1969, was a valiant attempt to make cruise and excursion shipping a viable enterprise on the lake, but it fell victim to harsh economic realities. The owner made one last attempt to stay in business by requesting permission for a casino that would operate only on the lake. That idea might well have worked, but it was an idea before its time and the provincial government turned the request down. The vessel now rests in "the slough" at Selkirk, the final resting place for several ships.

There are no cruise ships on Lake Winnipeg anymore and there haven't been since the *Lord Selkirk II* went out of service. There are still evening dinner/dance trips on the Red River, but the era of Lake Winnipeg cruises is long past. Today, Lake Winnipeg, with its unpredictable temper and its reputation of being a bad place to get caught in during a storm, is largely the home of fishing and pleasure boats.

How Winnipeggers Used to Frolic

The Elk's Jazz Band, popular in their day, enjoyed performing as much as their audiences enjoyed listening to them.

ARCHIVES OF MANITOBA (N1888)

At the turn of the twentieth century, most working people had neither the time nor the money to travel, even for a weekend, to exotic places such as the beaches of Lake Winnipeg. Vacations were almost unheard of at the time. As a result, Winnipeg, at one point a century ago, was home to not one, but three amusement parks.

The first two parks came into existence when Albert W. Austin started a horse-drawn tramway system. Faced with competition from another company operating electric streetcars, he built an electric streetcar line from the vicinity of the junction of the Red and Assiniboine Rivers, out to the south end of Osborne Street and along the Red River, parallel to what is now Jubilee Avenue. He believed that the city's growing population would soon occupy land in that area. But until subdivisions were surveyed and sold, Austin had to drum up business for his new route, so the Elm Park and River Park amusement centres came into being.

Elm Park, situated where Kingston Row now runs, was reached from the tram line by a pontoon bridge. It opened on 1 July 1891, with two thousand people in attendance. River Park opened shortly after, and on the Queen's Birthday, 25 May 1892, large crowds flocked to the city's newest fun places on Austin's cars. Some estimate as many as five thousand people went to the parks on that date. By that time River Park boasted a dance hall, where a band played on a number of weekend summer evenings.

However, Austin's horse-drawn cars in the downtown area couldn't compete with the electric vehicles, and, late in 1894, he sold out to William McKenzie and James Ross, the men who brought modern mass transit to Winnipeg. The two systems—McKenzie and Ross's downtown electric cars and Austin's electric line to the parks—were joined and passengers could travel the city on one system.

A couple of entrepreneurs named Darby and Sharp took over management of the amusement centres. One of their first innovations was a 21.3-metre by 51.8-metre (70-by-170-foot) roller skating rink, which offered twelve hundred pairs of skates for rent, a cement floor, a

Fun for All at Happyland

By 1906 River Park and Elm Park had been operating successfully in Winnipeg for almost fifteen years. The city was in the grip of a growing spell—the start of a boom. It was only natural that a group of Winnipeg businessmen should think that another amusement park couldn't help but succeed. On 1 May 1906 the Happyland Park Company was organized with a capital of $150,000.

Construction of the park began on the property between Aubrey and Dominion Streets, running from Portage Avenue all the way to the Assiniboine River. Happyland was promoted as the most modern amusement park in Canada. Publicity handouts stressed the athletic grounds complete with grandstand, picnic grounds and children's playground, a dance hall, and daycare provided by trained nurses.

Happyland also boasted Chateau Alphonse, a "crazy house" in which, according to legend, a scenic painter named C. P. Miller became lost when he tried to solve its maze-like mysteries one day after work. He not only had to spend the night there but also had to endure waiting for his rescuers, who searched for him by wandering aimlessly around the maze of corridors.

The park had the usual midway with all kinds of booths, a merry-go-round, and places to eat or to buy ice cream and other goodies. There was also a Japanese tea garden, the Old Mill with a boat ride through dark and mysterious tunnels, and "the smallest steam railway in the world," running on a track with a span of one foot. High over everything else at the park arose the outlines of the circular swing, 24.5 metres (80 ft.) high, and a massive roller coaster.

Thousands turned out on opening day, 23 May 1906. The weather wasn't fantastic, but the thousands of lights outlining the buildings made a great display, especially after dark. The grandstand was packed for a baseball game in which the Winnipeg Maroons were beaten by Duluth, seven to five—the defeat was blamed on the umpire. The game was the start of the Maroons' history as a professional team, part of the Northern Copper Country League.

The dance hall at Happyland, with a floor suspended on cushions to provide extra bounce for the dancers, was quite popular. But it was only open in the evenings, and even the presence of a woman described as "a real gypsy queen once loved by an English earl" was not sufficient to draw the crowds to make the enterprise truly profitable.

Mother Nature dealt Happyland a serious setback on 10 August 1907, when a storm of exceptional severity hit Winnipeg. Power and lights were off for several hours and many of Happyland's canvas and wood structures were damaged. Making matters worse, some circus animals also escaped from a sideshow that day. In an article for the Winnipeg Free Press, historian Edith Patterson recounted the surprise of a "spooning" couple on a veranda swing at a nearby house when a friendly young elephant wrapped its trunk around the young suitor's neck.

Financing problems dealt Happyland a crippling blow, and on 20 August 1908, the park went bankrupt. It was announced the property was to be sold at auction. Another local syndicate came forward and acquired Happyland—built at a cost of $150,000—for a mere $6,000.

From then on it was all downhill. The new owners advertised that Happyland's 1909 season would be the best

Fun for All at Happyland (cont.)

ever, and the park did, indeed, open in the spring of that year featuring a beer garden in the German style. But the hoped-for customers simply didn't come, and that was the end of the enterprise.

From 1909 to 1922, parts of the *high board fence that extended along the defunct amusement park's frontage still bore the huge faded lettering "Happy-land," along with barely decipherable phrases of all the delights that resort had offered.*

canvas roof, ladies' and gentlemen's waiting rooms, and "gentlemanly attendants," according to the advertisements.

At first Darby and Sharp added many new attractions to keep the customers coming. Ice cream and other refreshments were available, and a small zoo was established with domestic animals at first, but it was later expanded to contain bears and buffalo. The major attraction was the "Electric Riding Academy," with twenty-six horses, two six-seat chariots with a pictorial centre, and music provided by a band and an automatic organ with sixteen selections. It was just a merry-go-round, of course, but the high-sounding name must have been a greater lure.

Season tickets to either of the parks cost seventy-five cents for ladies and a dollar for gentlemen. There was a family rate of two dollars.

The big attraction for 1895 was Professor Menier, a daring balloon-ist, who was hired to ascend from the park in his balloon and descend again by parachute. He performed this feat in addition to his other accomplishment of diving from a high platform into the river.

By 24 May 1900, not one, but two "professors"—Thompson and Sandoff—were on hand to perform ascents, parachute jumps, fireworks from balloons, trapeze acts, slack-wire walks, and high dives. Unfortu-nately, the wind was too strong for ballooning, and the trapeze artist fell and broke his leg.

Under the management of John Hammerton, an early form of motion pictures projected by the Edison Kinetograph was shown, featur-ing footage from the Spanish–American War in 1899 and the Boer War in 1900. Customers could test their strength and win a cigar, watch the Winnipeg Maroons play baseball, attend horse races, or watch a stage show in the open air. They could also feed peanuts to the bears, which were kept in pits in the ground surrounded by both a spiked fence and a wire fence.

In 1906 the short-lived Happyland Park opened in competition with River and Elm Parks, but it was bankrupt within three years (see sidebar, "Fun for All at Happyland").

On hot summer days, particularly on weekends, the Winnipeg Electric Railway put its open cars into service on several city lines. These cars had the wheels, mechanism, and floor of a regular tram, but above that, there was only a roof supported on metal uprights. For thousands of kids who grew up in Winnipeg from the late 1890s to 1930, a highlight of their young lives was a ride on the wonderful open-sided cars to River Park.

A later addition to River Park's attractions was a roller coaster that, according to the myths of the time, was the biggest, fastest, and most exciting in North America. While a far cry from today's roller coasters, it must have been pretty good because when River Park was subdivided after the Second World War, the roller coaster was taken apart and shipped to San Diego, California, where it operated for a number of years.

Another of the park's memorable features was the toboggan slide complex on the riverbank south of Jubilee Avenue. For a quarter you could own a long toboggan for the evening; you climbed to the top of a tall timber tower, seated yourself, and were launched on a wild ride down a shallow chute coated with ice. The slide ended near the foot of another similar tower that took riders back to their starting place.

As time went on, Elm and River Parks faded into the background, and by the 1940s the land on which they had entertained thousands of Winnipeggers began to be developed for homes.

River Park and Elm Park—the names don't mean much now, but for several generations of Winnipeggers they were synonymous with a few hours of relaxation and that carnival atmosphere beloved of almost everyone now and then, and all for a tram ride and a few cents for admission.

The St. Peter's Land Struggle

A view of St. Peter's reserve (formed in 1871) as it was in 1884, before the questionable land deal of 1907 forced the Natives to give up this valuable land and move the reserve.

Seven years after the death of Peguis, the Saulteaux chief who had befriended and aided the Selkirk settlers, the province of Manitoba came into existence. Dealings with the Native peoples came under the control of Ottawa, and preparations were made for the signing of treaties and the creation of Indian reserves.

The Indian village around St. Peter's Church became St. Peter's Reserve under the terms of a treaty signed on 3 August 1871, and effective management passed from the hands of the Anglican missionaries who had founded the settlement in which, it was hoped, the Saulteaux would learn to become farmers.

The village had consisted of the church, mission house, school, and a couple of dozen Indian houses along the riverbank on both sides of Cook's Creek. The land was well treed but good quality farmland and, for more than thirty years, the Indians had lived there. However, from 1871 to 1885, there were numerous complaints from the Métis, who were also living in the area, that what they called "their property" had been turned over to the Indians.

The Métis' claim was settled in 1885 when a board of commissioners ruled that only those who had lived on and cultivated land in the area would be entitled to ownership. Among the Indians on the reserve was the Asham family, who were originally Swampy Cree from the area of The Pas, and who had come south in an effort to improve their condition and escape the poverty brought by over-trapping in the north.

By 1902 Chief Peguis' grandson, Reverend William Henry Prince, became chief of the St. Peter's Reserve and, during his time in office, the question of moving the band was hotly debated.

In mid-September 1907, four posters appeared in the village calling a meeting of all male members of the band over the age of twenty-one "for the purpose of considering, deciding, and assenting to the release and surrender of St. Peter's Indian Reserve on the terms to be set forth at the meeting." The notice was signed by Chief William Prince.

The posters appeared on 21 September, and the meeting was to be held on 23 September. When the appointed time arrived it was found that, although many reserve residents were absent hunting or fishing, so many turned up for the meeting they could not all fit into the tiny schoolhouse chosen as the meeting place.

William Asham, a band councillor who was part of the family that had come down from The Pas, left a full and literate account of the meeting. He had been asked to act as interpreter, as many of the Indians spoke no English, but he refused, wanting to have a free hand in the discussions.

The terms offered by Ottawa were that, for surrendering their claim to approximately 48,000 acres (19,425 hectares) of land, the band would receive five thousand dollars toward the cost of moving; the chief would get just under 180 acres (73 hectares), councillors 120 acres (48.6 hectares), and each Indian 16 acres (6.5 hectares).

Asham opposed the large differences in the sizes of the land grants, but, he wrote, "as the agreement of surrender was already prepared there was no change made at the time." He also claimed that two-thirds of the band present did not understand what the proposal meant. After some hours of discussion, he demanded a vote be taken.

"At this time," he wrote, "there was no question that a large majority of the band present were against the surrender and expressed themselves loudly to this effect."

The government representatives present refused to allow a vote but, when the meeting reconvened the next day, Asham said some of the surrender opponents had changed their minds. He reported, with names and details of conversation, the efforts of two representatives to bribe him with offers of land to change his mind. He refused.

Indian Affairs Deputy Superintendent Frank Pedley then pointed to a satchel at his side and said, according to Asham: "I have $5,000 here. If you agree to surrender to this, money will be distributed among you, but if you don't agree to the surrender, I will take my satchel and go home and you won't get a cent."

The meeting was then told it was time to take a vote, and because there were so many people present, the counting was done outside the school.

When the people assembled to place their votes, John Semmons, who was both the Indian agent and Anglican missionary on the reserve, shouted in a wild voice, in Cree, "All you that want $90 go to that side." Asham wrote that he was sure, in spite of Semmons' remark, that there was still a majority opposed, but when he had counted the number of those against the surrender, he was told that the pro-surrender side had been counted and had a majority of seven. He protested Semmons's phrasing of the shouted instructions, claiming the agent should have said, "All you that want to surrender the reserve go to one side."

The surrender document was then read rapidly, in English, and signed by the band chief and councillors. Opponents to the decision put the matter before the Member of Parliament for Selkirk, G. H. Bradbury, who pursued the matter in the House of Commons.

At the 1910 session of Parliament, Bradbury's speech on the surrender occupied fifty-three pages of *Hansard*, during which he charged that the land of St. Peter's Reserve had been the subject of speculation by "party-heelers" and was being resold to new settlers for eight to ten times what had been paid to the Indians.

On 14 October 1907 a federal order-in-council accepted the surrender, but four years later, Asham and sixty members of the St. Peter's band petitioned the premier of Manitoba, challenging the validity of the action and asking that no titles for the land be issued to purchasers until the whole matter had been investigated. The Manitoba registrar of titles refused to issue titles as Asham and his colleagues had asked.

No doubt this produced a spate of protests from purchasers of the former reserve land and from the provincial authorities because, in March 1908, Ottawa appointed a commission to probe into the whole surrender situation and to report to the government. This was carried out with surprising speed; within a few weeks two of the three commissioners presented a report that characterized the entire surrender as completely invalid and void.

Matters drifted along—with continued protests from some of the former St. Peter's residents—until May 1916, when Parliament passed the St. Peter's Reserve Act, legalizing the transaction, whereupon the Manitoba registrar commenced to issue titles for the former reserve land to its new owners. Those who had occupied the St. Peter's Reserve moved to the Peguis Reserve.

The exodus from St. Peter's to the Peguis Reserve on the Fisher River took some time. Land had to be cleared and broken, and houses built, and a long struggle ensued for amenities such as a school, a post office, and roads.

The controversy was papered over by a population of new Manitobans whose sole concern, as far as Indians went, was that they should stay out of sight for as long as possible.

Canada's Forgotten Pilot

Fred Stevenson, pioneer pilot, takes possession of copies of the
Winnipeg Evening Tribune *for delivery in northern*
Ontario. The aircraft is a Fokker Universal.

Does anyone remember Fred Stevenson? Want a clue? He was educated in Winnipeg, although his birthplace was Parry Sound, Ontario, and he regarded Winnipeg as his hometown. He was acknowledged as "Canada's premier commercial pilot."

Fred Stevenson was also the man for whom Winnipeg's airport was originally named, way back in the days when it was considered a good idea to call aerodromes after pioneering aviators. Today, it's just dull old Winnipeg International Airport, frighteningly interchangeable with any other airport in the world. In many American cities, airports still bear the names of local or national notables, and no one seems to worry about the possibility of people not knowing where the airport is. Today, only old-timers know what you're talking about when you say "Stevenson Field."

Stevenson was born in Parry Sound on 2 December 1895. His family moved to Winnipeg when he was small, and, like so many other Winnipeg youngsters, he went on to Wesley College (now the University of Winnipeg) after he completed high school.

His academic career didn't last long. The First World War was raging in Europe and, at the age of nineteen, Fred Stevenson quit school to join the army—the 196th University Battalion—and was shipped over to Britain. By 1917, however, he had managed to get a transfer to the Royal Flying Corps (RFC), the forerunner of the Royal Air Force.

His sister, Anne, remembered him as a big, healthy, enthusiastic fellow. He was unfazed by innovations and enjoyed new ideas and challenges. However, she wrote that Stevenson always told his family he had moved to the RFC "because the meals were better than we got in the army."

He went on squadron service and by the time the war ended had shot down eighteen enemy aircraft and destroyed three balloons. He was awarded the Distinguished Flying Cross, the French *Croix de Guerre*, and the Belgian *Croix de Guerre*.

Stevenson stayed with the Royal Air Force (as the service was renamed in 1918) for a few months after peace broke out, ferrying peace conference officials between London and Paris. But this was humdrum work, and when he was offered a job as a flying instructor for one of the anti-Bolshevik armies engaged in the Russian Civil War, he jumped at the chance.

The White Russian forces didn't fare very well after a few initial successes. Almost the only tangible memento of his Russian adventure was another decoration, the Order of St. Stanislaus, bestowed on him by the soon-to-be-defeated commander of the army he was serving.

Stevenson was back in Winnipeg by 1920, flying for the Canadian Aircraft Company, which bought seven Avro biplanes from England and used them for summertime tours of the province. Stevenson and his colleagues planned their itineraries to cover as many small towns as possible, their visits frequently coinciding with local fairs.

Frank Ellis, a pioneer pilot and mechanic of that time, part of Stevenson's group, and author of *Canada's Flying Heritage*, coined the word "farmstorming" to describe these tours. On arrival at a suitable field near the town, the pilots advertised they were ready and willing to take up passengers at a price of ten dollars for a ten-minute ride.

Ellis recalled that, very often, the visit of the flying circus was seized upon as an excuse for a community dance. On one such occasion at Treherne, Ellis and Stevenson were invited to the affair. "Unfortunately," Ellis wrote, "we had only the clothes we stood in, which, through much contact with oil and dust, were most unpresentable, Steve's [Stevenson's] being particularly grimy. With his gracious manner and his good dancing, however, he was extremely popular with the young ladies. As the evening wore on, it was easy to spot the girls he had danced with; their flowing white dresses showed the smudges transferred from his dirty flying togs."

Stevenson and Ellis ran into bad luck at Fort Francis, Ontario, in August 1920, when engine failure caused a crash from which Ellis walked away. But Stevenson suffered a broken jaw, a dislocated hip, and a broken ankle that left him with a permanent limp.

His injuries prevented him from flying for some time but, by 1924, Stevenson was back, flying forestry patrols for the Ontario Provincial Air Service out of Sault Ste. Marie and Sioux Lookout. Then, in 1926, he joined a legendary group headed by H. A. "Doc" Oakes—Western Canada Airways Ltd (WCA).

Working for WCA meant a new dimension in flying for Stevenson. The company hauled heavy freight—something never before attempted by air—for the Hudson Bay Railway then under construction, and for several mining companies that were opening in northern Manitoba.

His colleagues were men who later became world famous for their own flying exploits—men like Bernt Balchen and Al Cheesman. They were the trailbreakers for everything that has happened in northern aviation since then. A 1927 government report credited the company's success in flying unusual cargo to places where there were no facilities of any sort with the decision that Churchill should be the HB Railway terminus rather than York Factory.

Another milestone in northern flying was Stevenson's successful undertaking to fly 30.5 tonnes of heavy machinery from The Pas to the site of R. J. Jowsey's new Sherritt-Gordon mine in Lynn Lake.

Stevenson met his end, not on some perilous journey into the unknown north, but on a simple test flight at The Pas on 5 January 1928. His Fokker Universal plane spun into the ground, killing Stevenson instantly.

Two honours came to Stevenson posthumously. He was awarded the Harmon International Trophy for outstanding service to aviation, and the new airport at Winnipeg was named after him. His mother and father took part in a ceremony at the airport on 27–28 May 1928, when they unveiled a marble plaque commemorating their son's accomplishments.

In 1974 the vintage aircraft display and parade square at 17 Wing, Canadian Forces Base Winnipeg was named Stevenson Park, and an aviation technician training program located in Winnipeg and Portage la Prairie is called the Stevenson Aviation and Aerospace Training Centre. Perhaps some day, someone will reinstate the airport's original name, making one move at least to rescue Winnipeggers from grey uniformity.

Manitoba's Golden Boy

The Golden Boy was hoisted to the top of the Manitoba Legislative Building on 21 November 1919.

"The Golden Boy stands at the great meeting point of the East and the West, the North and the South, the old and the new . . . Winnipeg has caught the great idea of a city of humanity . . . All her busy life transpires under the gleam of the Golden Boy." Those are the words of a writer for the *Manchester News* who visited Winnipeg in 1947 and was, obviously, mightily impressed.

In spite of the fact he is balanced on one foot atop the legislative building dome, the Golden Boy stands firmly in place, both in fact and in the minds of Manitobans. He is instantly recognizable and is known to everyone who has ever lived in or visited Winnipeg. The Golden Boy is a true landmark. His early life, however, was considerably more precarious than his present exalted perch. In fact, he almost didn't get up there at all.

Before the First World War, the Manitoba government decided to construct a new building for the legislature and offices. A competition for the best design was held. The winner, Frank Simon of England, included a statue above the dome in his proposal, though nothing in the record shows whether he actually influenced the design of the figure.

In a separate contest to find the best statue design, a concept by Leonard Stokes, president of the Royal Institute of British Architects, was chosen. The man to whom the creation of the actual statue was entrusted was Georges Gardet of Paris, who also sculpted the gigantic bison that guard the legislature's grand staircase.

Gardet's statue was sent to the famous La Fonderie Barbidienne, a short distance from Paris, where it was cast in bronze early in 1918. Its design was based upon the sixteenth-century sculpture of Mercury by Giovanni da Bologna.

The statue was scarcely finished before a last-gasp offensive of the German army brought them near the French capital. The foundry was shattered by either bombs or shellfire; when the smoking ruins were examined, the only thing left undamaged was the Golden Boy. The statue was rushed to Le Havre and put on board a ship. This vessel was commandeered to carry war supplies and troops, so the young statue went on two Mediterranean trips and at least two trans-Atlantic crossings before

172

it was transported to its Canadian home. The statue, deep in the hold, made for excellent ballast and no one had the time to unload it, anyway.

Finally, the well-travelled Golden Boy was taken ashore in New York and shipped on a railway flatcar to Winnipeg, arriving in August 1919. Construction of the legislative building had started six years earlier, generating a scandal involving the awarding of contracts that toppled the government of Sir Rodmond Roblin in 1915.

On 21 November 1919 the Golden Boy was set in place under the anxious eye of Floyd E. (Buck) Buckham, an international expert in such work (see sidebar, "The Landmark Business of Buck Buckham").

Available records shed no light on the actual cost of the Golden Boy, however, the Public Works Department reports between 1916 and 1921 suggest a figure totalling $13,240.73. It is not known how much Gardet was paid for his work, nor how much it cost to transport the statue across the ocean—multiple times.

For the next thirty years, the Golden Boy weathered Manitoba's heat and cold, rain and snow, smoke and fumes. The original burnished bronze became dulled and mottled, and efforts to clean it never lasted long.

One such cleaning attempt resulted in a labour dispute. In 1948 two men won the contract for cleaning the statue. One said he would do the job up to the neck. The other—apparently an eye, ear, nose, and throat man—was to do the head. Errick Willis, onetime public works minister and later lieutenant-governor of Manitoba, described the events: "The body man finished his work, but when the head man was to start, his colleague refused to hold the ladder for him. The man who was to do the head went on strike; the other man also went on strike, perhaps in sympathy. It took several hours of negotiation by the [then] deputy minister, George Collins, to settle the matter and get it finished."

In 1951 the province decided to cover the statue with gold leaf, which is long lasting and resistant to discolouration. The contract was given to Baxter Signs, and Eric Hunt, an expert in this type of work, was assigned to the job.

Hunt erected scaffolding and swathed the Golden Boy in canvas while the work was in progress. Since application of the thin, almost transparent sheets of pure gold require a constant temperature and the work was being done in October, heaters were installed under the canvas. After several weeks, the Golden Boy was once more revealed, brilliant and shining.

About 32 square metres (50,000 sq. in.) of gold leaf were used to

The Landmark Business of Buck Buckham

Floyd E. Buckham—"Buck" to his friends—was an expert in just about anything to do with steel construction. During his lifetime he worked in all but one of the continental United States and in almost every province of Canada, putting up the basic skeletons of buildings, bridges, railroads, and even such exotic structures as Ferris wheels.

Buckham was born in 1870 in Rockport, Missouri. His father, Andrew, came from Scotland. As a teenager Buck spent school holidays working for one of his uncles on cattle drives. By age 19 he had graduated to learning steel construction techniques, working on bridges in the American Midwest and West. In 1892 he helped erect the giant Ferris wheel for the World Exposition in Chicago, and from 1895 to 1896 he worked on the building of Chicago's Northside Elevated Railway.

He spent years shuttling back and forth across the continent, building bridges in Pennsylvania and Virginia, a steel pier in Newport News, a warehouse in Connecticut, another elevated railway in Boston, and a bridge over the Colorado River for the Santa Fe Railroad.

His first major Canadian job was the Drummondville Bridge in Quebec in 1903. From there, he and his wife moved on to Galt, Ontario, for a powerhouse contract, then to Guelph for an aluminum company job, and then to Alberta to build a bridge. In 1907 the Buckhams came to Winnipeg and made it their permanent home. That year Buck was in charge of all the steelwork involved in the construction of the Bank of Montreal building at the corner of Portage and Main.

Those were the days, as Buckham noted in his memoirs, when paperwork was at a minimum and agreements to perform the complex and demanding work he undertook were sealed by a handshake instead of by pages of documentation.

From 1908 to 1909 Buck worked on the steel frame for the railway depot at the end of Broadway Avenue on Main Street and also on the CN Shops in Transcona. He later built the skeleton of the Orpheum Theatre—and also worked on the dismantling of that landmark. He put up the subway span over Water Street for the CNR and was involved in the building of the intake structure for the Greater Winnipeg Water District at Shoal Lake.

However, the most obvious of all Buckham's contracts in Winnipeg was the Golden Boy statue above the legislative building. Buckham was given the contract to place it on its lofty pedestal. But first he had to construct a long circular staircase inside the dome so that his work crews could gain access to the top of the dome.

Placing the statue on its perch high above the ground called for ingenious innovations and a large web of scaffolding around the dome. The hoisting of the Golden Boy took place all in one day, 21 November 1919.

After completing this project, Buckham helped erect the First World War memorial at the corner of Portage and Main.

His last professional contract was the construction of a large derrick at Riverton, for Riverton Airways in 1965, when he was in his mid-nineties.

Floyd Buckham died in 1968. Speaking of his style of working and living, Buckham once said, "I guess I must have had some sand in my craw. I never backed away from a hard man or a hard job."

cover the Golden Boy. That sounds like a lot, but it only represents about five to seven ounces of twenty-three-karat gold. Ron D. Turner, provincial treasurer in 1951, said it was worth about the same as the price of a medium-sized car—no more than three thousand dollars.

From a distance the Golden Boy seems rather small, but in fact his dimensions are quite impressive. He is 4.1 metres (13.5 ft.) from toe to crown of head—or 4.9 metres (16 ft.) to the top of the torch in his raised hand. The tip of the torch is 68.6 metres (255 ft.) above ground level. His body measurements are: chest, 243.8 centimetres (96 in.); neck, 89 centimetres (35 in.); arm and thigh, both 132.1 centimetres (52 in.); waist, 193 centimetres (76 in.); and calf, 96.5 centimetres (38 in).

For those whose duty calls them to reach the statue, access is not easy. There's a winding stairway that circles between the inner and outer shells of the dome. An unmarked door leads to a stairway that gives entry to a large room directly below the statue, a room that is about 9 metres high (30 ft.) and has a floor space of 279 square metres (3,000 sq. ft.). There is another spiral stair, then a hatch leading to the foot of the Golden Boy. From that point, a ladder or scaffolding is required to go any higher.

A torch was added to the statue to mark Canada's Centennial in 1967. Workmen clamped a seventy-five-watt mercury vapour lamp into the torch, and the light was first switched on at 3 PM on 31 December 1966.

The torch shone out brightly until 2002 when the need for major repairs to the pin holding the Golden Boy in place required the statue to be lowered to the ground for the first time since 1919. After being put on display at the Museum of Man and Nature in Winnipeg, where ninety thousand people came to see him, the statue was taken apart and refurbished. A new layer of gold leaf was applied before he was returned to his perch. On 8 October 2002, Queen Elizabeth II presided over the ceremony to relight his torch.

The legislative building's architect, Frank Simon, wrote: "Here, you have no mountains to which you can lift up your hearts. And so you have all the more need of great architecture to which you can lift them up. Manitoba and Winnipeg cannot be happy and good in surroundings that are commonplace, ugly or uninspiring."

Certainly the Golden Boy, after all his early trials, travels, and exposure to decades of harsh climate, and despite the ever-changing political landscape below his feet, shines against the prairie sky as an enduring symbol of faith and hope.

The Strike to
End All Strikes

*Mounted police gather at the corner of Portage and
Main during the Winnipeg General Strike, 21 June 1919.*

In times of peace and times of crisis, the mayor and aldermen of any municipality must make what they think are the appropriate decisions for their city. During periods of unrest, the decisions made by one mayor and council can have far-reaching implications not only for their particular city but also for whole regions and economies. One man who filled the mayor's position during a period of great social and political turmoil in Winnipeg was Charles Frederick Gray, who presided over the affairs of the city for two terms from 1919 to 1920. In Manitoba, if not all of western Canada, the year 1919 was dominated by one event—the Winnipeg General Strike.

For six weeks almost all the normal activities of the city came to a halt as more than thirty thousand people quit work—machinists, public transport workers, postal workers, bankers, delivery men, telegraphers, bakers, dairy workers, and even the police went on strike. Gray had only held the mayoralty for a few months when this crisis occurred, but he brought to his post a background of experience with hard times and adventure.

He was born in London, England, in 1879. At the age of thirteen, he ran away to sea, shipping aboard a pilot cutter in North Wales. His parents apparently realized he could do worse than to get some real-life experience, for at the age of fourteen, they signed him on as an apprentice aboard the clipper ship *Oronsay*, aboard which he made three trips around the world. One of these trips involved going to Cape Horn in wintertime—the world's worst passage in a sailing ship. As Gray described it, "the waves were one hundred feet high with half a mile between each wave." Before he was seventeen, Gray had experienced a mid-Atlantic shipwreck.

After his seafaring youth he became an electrical engineer and was sent by his employer, the Westinghouse Company, to Nelson, BC, to work on the new smelter there. Then he went back to England for a time and was involved in the electrification of the London Underground, but Westinghouse soon sent him back to Canada to install the generating equipment for City Hydro at Pointe du Bois. On completion of this project he settled in Winnipeg.

Gray was elected mayor in the municipal election of 1918 and took office at the beginning of 1919. One of his first duties was to try to settle a dispute between the metal trades workers and their employers—the major companies were Vulcan Iron Works, Manitoba Bridge and Iron, and Dominion Bridge. The unions wanted all the employers to negotiate with all the unions involved at the same time. The companies refused to do so and were opposed to collective bargaining.

By the time Gray was in office, the trade unions of Winnipeg—through their central organization, the Winnipeg Trades and Labour Council, and supported by a new organization, the One Big Union, and small but vocal socialist groups—were talking about a general strike.

The chief grievance was pay. After the First World War prices rose sharply and pay rates did not. Many people found they were falling further and further behind in providing the necessities of life, let alone thinking about luxuries or savings.

Along with provincial officials, Gray made a strong attempt to steer events toward negotiation. Some of the moderate union leaders were inclined to agree but, by that time, the trend toward strike action had gained a momentum. Fifty-two affiliated unions held a vote, and 11,112 union members voted for a work stoppage with only 524 against. Although Gray and Manitoba Premier T. C. Norris made several bids to conciliate the dispute, the strike started on 15 May 1919.

There was a body of opinion at all levels of government, especially the federal government, that some of the strike leaders were intent on seizing power and setting up a revolutionary government. It seems clear from all that has been said and written that such a program was in the minds of a few of the strike leaders, but they were in the minority.

Anticipating trouble, Ottawa moved detachments of the Royal Northwest Mounted Police (NWMP) into the city and placed troops at Fort Osborne barracks on alert.

One observer remarked that, after countless hours of meetings, the mayor "looked very much like a tired Liberal. He had early made sincere efforts at conciliation, but was bitterly criticized by both sides. The strikers regarded him as the tool of reaction, while the Citizens' Committee referred to him as a spineless accepter of revolution."

Gray managed to get the metal trade unions and their employers to agree to further bargaining but, in the meantime, warrants had been issued in Ottawa for the arrest of a dozen of the strike leaders.

Protest marches were organized. A Citizens' Committee of One Thousand had been formed in the city, and many of these were sworn in as special constables. Many soldiers newly returned from the war supported the strikers, largely because they had come home to find no jobs available. Other returned veterans, however, joined the Citizens' Committee and helped to police the city.

On 21 June a great demonstration in support of the strike and of the now-released leaders was called. Gray issued an order banning all demonstrations and called in the NWMP to break up the crowds already gathering on Main Street in front of city hall. He issued a clear warning that any attempt to hold a parade would be met with severe action.

An account of those events, printed in the *Winnipeg Tribune* of 25 March 1941, said that in his final meeting with ex-soldier supporters of the strike—who were demanding a parade—he turned to leave after repeating his ban on demonstrations. "At the door, he turned to warn the soldiers that the parade would be stopped by peaceful means if possible but if necessary by sterner measures." Gray then went to city hall just as the NWMP were forming up on Main Street to clear the thousands of people who filled the roadway.

Batons swinging, the police charged the crowd but failed to clear the street. On the steps of city hall, Gray read the Riot Act, which empowered civil authorities to use force to put down a disturbance threatening the peace of the community.

The police drew their guns and again charged, firing several volleys into the dense throng. A number of people fell, and the demonstrators, realizing the seriousness of the situation, began to disperse. Two men were killed, almost one hundred were wounded, and scores were arrested. Truckloads of troops with machine guns began to patrol Portage Avenue and Main Street.

The strike was over. The unions hurriedly decided to return to work although, in a number of cases, employers would not take back some of the employees who had walked out.

Gray was a central character in the investigation of the whole incident that followed and a key witness in the trials of the strike leaders who were charged with sedition, among other things.

When municipal elections came around again in the fall of 1919, Gray ran and was re-elected. Then, and later, he said he felt he had done all he could to bring about a peaceful settlement but added that when the strikers refused to call off their parades, which were creating "dangerous currents" in the city, he was forced to call in the NWMP and troops. He often said that those few weeks in 1919 changed the colour of his hair to match his name.

In 1941 Gray went to British Columbia to become general manager of a salt mine and refinery. He died in Victoria in 1954.

No Drinking Please, We're Manitobans

Strict liquor laws, which followed earlier times of heavy drinking, led to the creation of stills such as this one.

ARCHIVES OF MANITOBA (N2262)

When provincial liquor laws were changed in the late 1980s, enabling a number of watering holes to stay open an extra hour, many remembered the rules of an earlier era and the ways in which they were evaded.

More than a century ago, Winnipeg was noted for its saloons and bars and was once considered one of the "wickedest cities in Canada." The era of the saloon came to an end, however, with the enactment of prohibition laws during the First World War. The sale of liquor was thenceforth prohibited except for a few specific purposes. Paradoxically, manufacturing alcoholic beverages was permitted, giving rise to the highly illegal but equally highly profitable business of "rum running" from Canada to the United States, which was also experimenting with legislated sobriety.

The United States did not scrap prohibition until 1933 but, long before that, province by province, Canada abandoned the ideal. Quebec led the way in 1919, and, in 1923, a plebiscite in Manitoba empowered the provincial government to set up a monopoly for the sale of beer, wines, and spirits. At first only those Canadians over the age of twenty-one and in possession of a permit were allowed to buy booze. The permit gave the holder the privilege of buying a certain number of bottles of alcohol within a certain time period. The details of the sale had to be entered on the permit, which could be suspended or withdrawn if the holder showed signs of becoming a habitual drunk.

In addition, hotels were allowed to sell beer only in what were known as beverage rooms but were usually referred to as beer parlours. These were, for the most part, dreary places where one had to sit at a table and be served by waiters. There was no food, and drinkers could not consume their favourite quaff standing up, nor could they carry their drink from one table to another.

It was not until the 1950s that changes in the law were made, largely as a result of a provincial commission that carried out a far-reaching study of the existing laws and their relationship to public perceptions of drinking. This study was headed by former premier John Bracken and resulted in a total overhaul of the rules. Restaurants were permitted to serve beer, wine, and liquor, and cocktail bars or lounges were gradually introduced. However, in the period before this radical change, Winnipeggers found various ways, most of them unsubtle, of slipping between the iron fingers of the authorities in order to imbibe.

There were, of course, the bootleggers—people who either sold, or made and sold, various quantities of liquor. Some bootleggers handled standard brands of Scotch whisky, rye, gin, and so on, buying it from the government stores and retailing it after liquor store hours with a substantial markup. Others, frequently in isolated places in rural areas, brewed, fermented, and distilled beverages from a variety of basic materials such as grain and potatoes. Quality and price varied as did the length of time such entrepreneurs were able to evade the watchful eyes of the police. The usual penalty for brewing alcohol was a fine, but the profits were more than enough to satisfy the bootleggers, even allowing for the fines.

Of course, people also liked to get together in public places to socialize, to eat and dance, and, of course, to drink. A number of establishments opened in Winnipeg to provide the locale, the music, and the (token) food. The law, of course, made it necessary for the proprietors of such places to leave the matter of providing the drinks entirely up to the customers. Some of these so-called nightclubs appeared and quickly disappeared, but others enjoyed long and memorable lives.

One of the earlier places that did business in the 1920s was located on the south side of the Assiniboine River near where the Headingley Bridge crosses. It was called Dixieland and was in an old white house with a porch and a large front yard. A sign consisting of electric light bulbs spelled out the name and, for a time, this was *the* place to go to party.

Another of the popular nightclubs was the Kit Kat Klub, located in an old store out in the area then known as Sturgeon Creek, a long way west from St. James Street, which was then the western boundary of the city of Winnipeg. A little farther in toward the city was Duke's Dine and Dance, a long one-storey building with the inevitable flashing sign.

Within the city there were several clubs, once well-known landmarks. Some were quite respectable places, and others were known for rowdiness and frequent police attention. On Pembina Highway, for instance, there was Jack's Place at the junction of the highway and Regina (now University) Crescent. The Highwayman was located a little farther north. There was the Cave at the corner of Ellice Avenue and Princess Street, and there were hangouts with colourful names like the Blue Danube, the Aragon, the Trianon, and the Lido.

The Cave was perhaps the best known of the establishments that provided glasses, ice, and mixers at a cost. The entire interior of the public area was, by the artful use of *papier maché*, framework, and dim lighting, transformed into a cave, or series of caves. Marsh Phimister and his band played there for many years, and the customers behaved with relative propriety—relative compared to what went on in some of the less savoury joints.

How did the partiers of those days get around the liquor laws? Well, it was a case of "bring your own bottle"—in a brown paper bag, stashed under the table throughout the evening, and only brought out for careful and surreptitious pourings of drinks into glasses supplied along with ice and mixers by the management of the place, at a considerable profit.

Everybody, including the authorities, knew what was going on at these clubs. But a certain segment of the population felt a need for places where they could go to drink with others and, for the most part, those charged with enforcing the liquor laws turned a blind eye. The more respectable places were checked, now and then, and every so often a token arrest or two was made. But these were few and far between.

Today there's hardly a restaurant that doesn't have a licence to serve wine or beer at least, and there are many people patronizing such places today who don't realize that there was a time when strict laws prevailed on drinking.

The Messengers
of St. Faith's

Transportation to church for a member of
St. Faith's, Easter 1937.

(WITH PERMISSION OF THE GENERAL SYNOD ARCHIVES,
ANGLICAN CHURCH OF CANADA)

After the First World War, from 1919 to 1926, many Canadian army veterans and a considerable number of ex-servicemen from Britain settled in the Swan River Valley of Manitoba and areas farther north. With limited resources, these men went into what was then frontier land with the intention of farming. Some were single, some brought wives and families and, for a considerable number, the transition to the wild and lonely bush country was an eye-opener.

Some simply could not cope with the combination of isolation and the difficulties of breaking and clearing land and building shelter. Others struggled on and by the late 1920s were beginning to see some results for their efforts.

One of the things these pioneers lacked, and for which they felt a need, was some form of religious organization and service. Travel in the recently settled areas was difficult and farms were scattered. As a result these men and women rarely saw anyone connected with a church.

Around this time a well-educated English woman was looking for a project that would fulfill her desire to be of service. Marguerita Fowler had cared for her elderly mother and father until their deaths and had then gone to St. Christopher's College in Blackheath, London, where she took a two-year course that emphasized theology and social work.

After completing her course, she came to Canada in 1926 to visit friends in Winnipeg, where she heard about the hopes and needs of settlers in the Interlake and Swan River areas. One of the settlers she spoke to had been the gardener on her father's estate in England. He told her that he had not been to church since coming to Canada, mainly because of the lack of a church to attend.

Fowler's natural wish to do work of social significance and her training at St. Christopher's led her to suggest that she could organize and carry out some sort of rural mission within the Anglican Church.

While at St. Christopher's she had met Eva Hasell, who had worked in an organization that operated "caravan missions," travelling by bus to isolated areas where she organized Sunday schools. She had also organized a

Sunday school by mail. Hasell arranged for Fowler to visit Bishop Thomas of Brandon, who was enthusiastic about her idea for a rural mission.

Thus was formed an order of women to be called Messengers. Members of the order had to be more than twenty-three years old, in good health, and members of the Church of England. They had to take part in daily prayer and meditation, receive communion when possible, attend an annual retreat, and take part in housekeeping duties in their residence. Initially, members of the order wore a blue dress with a white cross on the front and a simple blue veil, although changes were later made to their attire.

As the Swan River Valley was the northern limit of the main settled area in the diocese, Bishop Thomas chose Swan River as the initial location for the order. Marguerita arrived in Swan River on 22 June 1926 with one other Messenger. There she established the order's Mother House and named it St. Faith's. Thereafter the Messengers became the Messengers of St. Faith's.

By 1928 there were five women in the order—Marguerita, Muriel Secretan, Margaret Robertson, Muriel Williamson, and Muriel Hooper—but over the lifetime of the order fifty-six women would be licensed as Messengers. Some of those who joined the order in the early days were Englishwomen who had lost their fiancés in the First World War and had decided to devote their lives to some form of social service.

Working from Swan River, the Messengers visited all the tiny communities within reach of their limited and varied methods of transportation—sleigh, car, truck, horseback, or on foot—and provided a wide variety of services besides religious teaching.

Gradually, as individuals and families in the valley heard of their work, and as the Messengers heard of people who needed help, they moved out, forming a network of religious and social interest. In many cases they started by getting the children interested in Sunday school and in enrolling them in the Sunday school-by-mail program. From this beginning, parents became involved. Within a few years, the Messengers had established a series of tiny congregations, encouraging faith, and providing help and encouragement to scores of families.

The Messengers had been well trained and were able to advise on matters of health as well as religion. They provided counselling wherever it was needed and were instrumental in helping many families over rough periods in their isolated lives.

They had been commissioned by the Bishop of Brandon, in whose diocese they were operating, to preach sermons, to baptize in emergencies, and to conduct funerals when no ordained priest could do so. Hence the women were commonly referred to as the "Bishop's Messengers." They had, in fact, all the authority of deacons in the Anglican Church.

Apart from the order's house in Swan River, the Messengers of St. Faith's worked from a wide and sometimes startling variety of accommodations. In Mafeking, for instance, they started holding services in the local hotel, the only place in town where there was enough room. However, the noise from the beer parlour was a definite drawback, and the Messengers finally rented a house in town from which to work.

The Bishop of Brandon assigned fully qualified members of the clergy to work with the Messengers and keep the diocesan office informed of their progress. One retired Anglican priest, Canon Laurence Wilmot, was chaplain of the Order of St. Faith's for seven years and visited the members on a regular basis.

One of the order's biggest challenges was in establishing a base in the town of Birch River, which was regarded as a "pagan town," Wilmot said in an interview. "Even the United Church had closed its doors." The Messengers went into Birch River, however, and enrolled many children in Sunday school and, in addition, organized Guides and Scouts groups. Then, to arouse interest and activity among adults, they arranged for a parade to march through the town with Girl Guides, Boy Scouts, and other youngsters stopping at every street corner to sing a hymn and to preach a short sermon.

After the parade the Birch River town school was filled to overflowing, and an active and enthusiastic congregation was organized. After an unsuccessful offer was made to buy the abandoned United Church, a new Anglican Church was soon under construction.

By 1959 the order saw a need for its services in The Pas and the area to the north of it. A St. Faith's house was established in The Pas, and missions were sent out to such centres as Cormorant Lake and Wabowden. In fact, there was so much to do in that area that the Messengers' headquarters was eventually moved to The Pas from Swan River. From The Pas, the travelling teams of Messengers went out to Grand Rapids, Cedar Lake, Moose Lake, Herb Lake, and Lynn Lake in Manitoba, and to Pelly in Saskatchewan.

At The Pas the order also established a halfway house for Native girls. At this house the order provided information about and leadership in the subjects of health, sanitation, and nutrition. As the Messengers moved into areas with larger Native populations, they became more and more concerned with the problems faced by Aboriginal peoples and spent a great deal of time and effort in working with and assisting them.

Among the secular activities for which the order was best known were shelters for battered wives, the development of low-cost housing projects, the supply of emergency food and clothing to those in need, and partnerships with child welfare organizations.

A number of the qualified Messengers taught or nursed in the districts where they were stationed, thus supplying welcome monies to the order's restricted funds. The order's statement of receipts and disbursements for 1969 gives a clear picture of their finances, showing an income of $5,988.24 and expenditures of $5,842.78.

By the 1970s the many changes taking place in the world, in the diocese, and in the church were reflected in the work onf the order. The need for many of its services had been met by other organizations. Also, the Anglican Church was on the verge of ordaining deaconesses and only a little further away from ordaining women as priests. The Messengers themselves realized what was happening, and on 27 December 1979 the Order of St. Faith's held its final meeting and voluntarily dissolved itself.

Its members had filled a great need. Dedicated, capable, and hardworking women had gone out into the pioneer districts, bringing help, faith, and hope to those who had almost forgotten such words existed. An Anglican priest who went into a parish served by the order until his appointment, considered their work as he had seen it and commented, "It was a hard act to follow."

High Arctic Survival

The MacAlpine party stands around at Cambridge Bay,
the northernmost point in their odyssey, with the
HBC ship Maude Bay *in the background.*

One of the great stories of Canadian aviation started and finished in Winnipeg when two aircraft lifted off from the Western Canada Airways base on the Red River.

It was 24 August 1929. The single-engine, float-equipped Fokker and Fairchild airplanes, one owned by Western Canada Airways, the other by Dominion Explorations, carried seven men. Their mission was to fly over more than 32,000 square kilometres (20,000 sq. mi.) of the largely unmapped and unknown Northwest Territories to prepare for later intensive searches for mineral bodies and other resources that could be developed. Earlier bush pilots had ventured as far north as Baker Lake and Chesterfield Inlet north of Churchill on Hudson Bay, and the 1929 party was to make use of the knowledge gained by these pilots.

The party included: Colonel C. D. H. MacAlpine, president of Dominion Explorations; Richard Pearce, editor of the *Northern Miner*; E. A. Boadway, a mining engineer; pilots G. A. Thompson and Stan McMillan; and aircraft engineers A. D. Goodwin and Alex Milne.

The two planes headed for Norway House, but their view of the ground was obscured in many areas by dense layers of forest fire smoke. The planes lost their way several times and had to land on Lake Winnipeg to find out where they were. In the early days of air travel, aircraft were not equipped with radios, and ground navigation aids such as radio beacons were virtually non-existent.

Arrangements had been made for the schooner *Morso* to bring gasoline, and other stores needed for the expedition, to Churchill. But on their arrival there, the explorers found the ship had not yet arrived. The day after the planes reached Churchill, two small boats entered the harbour, bearing the *Morso*'s crew. The ship had caught fire and blown up, taking all the expedition's supplies with it. Worse was to come.

The next day a storm dragged one of the planes from its moorings and drifted it out to sea where it sank. MacAlpine radioed to Winnipeg for a replacement, and part of the party went north to Baker Lake in the remaining aircraft.

A new plane, piloted by Roy Brown of Winnipeg, reached Churchill on 6 September, picked up the waiting expedition members, and took them to Baker Lake. The reunited team took off from there on 9 September. Because the proximity of the north magnetic pole rendered regular magnetic compasses unreliable, the team was using a relatively new instrument, the sun compass.

Their immediate goal was Bathurst Inlet, more than 640 kilometres (400 mi.) to the northwest, but their navigation was thrown off by violent storms. Finally, after more than five hours in the air, they landed on what they thought was part of Bathurst Inlet, but which later proved to be the northern coast of Canada, about 120 kilometres (75 mi.) east of their objective.

There was a small Inuit village near where they landed. It contained three inhabitants—a man, a woman, and a baby—who were unable to give the explorers an exact location, although they indicated a Hudson's Bay Company post was in a northwesterly direction.

Two days of bad weather followed, and a check of their fuel showed it was dangerously low. It was decided to put all the fuel into one of the planes for a flight over the sea in the hope of locating the HBC post. Bad visibility forced them to return, and they decided to make camp and wait for better conditions.

They built a sod hut and tried to use a tarpaulin to extend the hut's capacity, but it later caused trouble when rain and snow fell. The shelter measured 4.2-by-3.7-by-1.5 metres (14-by-12-by-5 ft.).

It was now 18 September, and each member of the party was worried, not so much for themselves—they knew where they were—but for their families, who didn't.

Three more Inuit arrived in the village on 20 September, bringing some food and welcome fur clothing. The party's rations had dwindled, particularly their tobacco stores into which their Inuit hosts had made great inroads. Meanwhile, the stranded men started to sample the Native food, but found it hard to eat, consisting as it did of very old fish.

They had guns and ammunition and managed to shoot a few ptarmigan and ground squirrels. They traded a pair of field glasses to one of the Inuit for a metal stove, enabling them to cook some of the food, but they were so tired of old fish that Richard Pearce offered his wristwatch to the first person to bring in some caribou. Two of the Inuit family finally brought in fresh fish and a large piece of freshly killed caribou, for which Pearce gladly surrendered his watch.

By the end of September twigs and driftwood for fuel were hard to come by, so they decided to drain the fuel tank of the plane into which they had poured their total supply. They were horrified to discover it contained only about a litre—if they hadn't turned back on that last flight, they would have fallen into the sea.

The Natives warned that it would be foolhardy to try to walk anywhere because of the weather and the fact that they would surely encounter open water. But by 20 October, the Inuit decided it was safe to travel, and the whole party set out across horrendous miles of piled-up sea ice and treacherous areas of thin ice.

They reached Cambridge Bay early on 3 November. An HBC ship, the *Bay Maud*, was wintering there and one of its crew managed to get a radio message about the expedition to another icebound ship, the *Fort James*, which then relayed it to Churchill. Meanwhile, six planes had started to search for the missing party (from a base at Baker Lake).

On 17 October, gale-driven ice damaged the tail of one of the search aircraft, and on 18 October, while landing to refuel at the supply cache at Burnside River, one of the planes went through thin ice and sank until only the top of the wing was showing. The crew escaped through the top hatch.

Then, as search crews were running up their engines on the morning of 5 November, someone spotted a dog team and driver travelling toward them at considerable speed. As he neared, the Inuit driver shouted, "They find 'em!" He carried a written message from the Bathurst radio operator and had travelled more than ten hours over rough terrain, and at night, to bring the news.

Plans were made to pick up the MacAlpine party at Cambridge Bay, but there was still trouble ahead. Three of the rescue planes were damaged from landings on rough ice, and the rescued MacAlpine party had to be flown in relays in the one usable plane. They got back to Winnipeg, via The Pas, on 4 December, 102 days after they had taken off from the Red River base.

"The Natives were lifesavers for us," said MacAlpine later. He left them his rifles and ammunition, sent them sewing machines, clothing, and tobacco, and left several hundred dollars with the Cambridge Bay post manager to the credit of those who assisted and supplied his group.

All in all, it was a remarkable feat—or series of feats—at a time when the north was truly a wilderness.

We Knew Our Rights

*Marcus Hyman was a member of the Manitoba Legislature
and author of the private member's bill that led to the first
human rights bill in Canada.*

Protests and lawsuits based on human rights legislation have become commonplace in recent years, creating the impression that laws protecting minorities are new. In fact, Manitoba's legislature passed a law protecting minorities in 1934—the Manitoba Defamation Act—which was the first of its kind in the country and, for thirty-six years, Canada's only such law.

The act was important because it allowed groups to launch legal action against anyone who was seen to commit libel against them. The law itself came about because of the political and emotional climate of the 1930s and the rise of authoritarian governments in Europe.

The Great Depression spawned many so-called "solutions" for the difficulties that beset the world. In western Canada the ever-present simmering of political and economic ideas came to a full rolling boil and produced new organizations, including Social Credit, the Co-operative Commonwealth Federation (CCF, later the New Democratic Party), and a number of minor organizations whose proposals failed to attract more than a mere handful of supporters.

The examples of Fascist Italy and Nazi Germany didn't escape the notice of people who were disenchanted with the prevailing order of things and who were, at the same time, inclined to muscular and authoritarian solutions. The largest and longest-lasting Canadian manifestation of the Fascist phenomenon occurred in Quebec, where Adrien Arcand's National Social Christian Party was formed in 1934.

Winnipeg looked like an excellent breeding ground for the creed of racial hatred and violent action that had succeeded in Germany. A very considerable Jewish community flourished in the city, and a high percentage of the population was either from eastern and central Europe, or descended from recent immigrants from those regions.

In addition to appealing to Canadians of German origin, Nazi emissaries tried to make capital of the strong anti-Communist sentiments among some of those whose roots were in eastern Europe and who, in some cases, had personally experienced the events of the Russian Revolution.

Political and economic power was still largely in the hands of people of Anglo-Saxon origin, so the most visible Fascist-type group to emerge was made up at first of veterans of the First World War, led by an English ex-soldier and ex-policeman named William Whittaker.

On 26 September 1933 Whittaker founded the Canadian Nationalist Party. Clad in brown shirts, khaki breeches, and high boots, they vowed to fight Communism, to maintain allegiance to the monarch, and, their main goal, to abolish all provincial legislatures and make the federal government supreme in Canada. "With one national government, we could stop Communism," Whittaker said. According to him, Canada should have become a corporate state like Mussolini's Italy, though Whittaker offered no detailed programs for its realization.

Whittaker's newspaper, the *Canadian Nationalist*, was violently anti-Semitic. At meetings, uniformed members watched the audience and maintained order and some wore the swastika emblem.

Opponents of Fascism—most notably the local Communist organization, but also the Independent Labour Party and the trade unions—made strenuous efforts to offset the National Party propaganda. John Queen, Labour MLA and later mayor of Winnipeg, bitterly attacked Whittaker's party and paper in the legislature to the point that Attorney General W. J. Major was forced to make a strong statement upholding the rights of all minorities, claiming that any person or group who felt they had been wronged could obtain satisfaction through the law.

Major's statement was shortly tested when it was learned that anti-Fascists were going to try and break up an advertised Nationalist meeting. Major banned the meeting but then was on the horns of a dilemma: How free is freedom of speech and how far can government go in curtailing it without being dictatorial?

At the same time another Labour MLA, Marcus Hyman, introduced a private member's bill in the legislature that would give groups who felt they had been libelled the right to take the matter to court. Up until then libel actions could only be brought to court by individuals. The bill passed, and Manitoba's Defamation Act of 1934 became the first such legislation in Canada.

Meanwhile, the animosity between Whittaker's "Brown Shirts" and those opposed to them had grown. In June 1934 a full-scale riot broke out in Market Square, where the Public Safety Building now stands. Clubs and knives were in evidence, according to newspaper reports, and those without weapons tore chunks from the market gardeners' stalls to use against their political foes.

The Nationalists were outnumbered and came off second-best, with some of them needing hospital treatment. Nine of Whittaker's stalwarts were arrested and seven were charged with taking part in a riot. They were released on bail of one thousand dollars each. There never was any indication where the bail money—a vast sum in those lean Depression years—came from.

Whittaker died later that year, and while his party and paper remained active for some time in both Manitoba and Saskatchewan, they were never as prominent as they had been in the news.

Strong links between Germany and some members of the German-Canadian community in the west were forged by several men who were, apparently, sent here for the specific purpose of building pro-Nazi and pro-German sentiments. One of these men was a "professor," whose credentials later were proven to be false, who worked with some success both in Manitoba and in Montreal to gather support for Hitler's regime. Another was the German consul in Winnipeg, Dr. Seelheim, who wrote a number of vitriolic letters to the press in support of his homeland's policies.

The Deutsche Band, as the pro-Nazi organization in Canada and the United States was called, provided a good deal of support for movements like Whittaker's and, in fact, several writers from the 1930s have noted the extent to which Fascist and anti-Semitic sentiments were accepted by some Canadians.

In the end, however, all these organizations disappeared with the outbreak of the Second World War in 1939. Many, such as Adrien Arcand in Quebec, were interned along with, ironically, members of the Canadian Communist Party who had battled Fascism in the 1930s. The Communists were incarcerated in Canada, of course, because of the infamous pact signed between Fascist Germany and the Soviet Union.

Thanks to God
and the RCAF

The party that went missing on their arrival at The Pas, following their rescue. From left to right: USN *Chief Petty Officer Jack Kastner;* RN *Captain Sir Robert Stirling Hamilton;* USN *Captain Ben Scott Custer;* USN *Lt. Charles Wilcox;* US *Army Master Sergeant Jerome Scalise.*

WINNIPEG TRIBUNE, H.G. AIKMAN (GIVEN TO AUTHOR IN 1991)

It was a grim, dull day on 11 September 1948, with heavy overcast skies and occasional windblown showers, when two lean grey warships carefully nosed their way into harbour and tied up alongside the towering grain elevators. For the first time, the Royal Canadian Navy had arrived in Churchill, Manitoba.

Although the arrival of HMCS *Haida* and HMCS *Nootka* in the northern port was newsworthy enough to rate the presence of a number of reporters and photographers, it was just the prelude to an even bigger news story that commanded front-page attention in Canada, the United States, and Britain.

Nootka and *Haida* had been part of a naval force conducting an Arctic exercise. On their way through Hudson Bay, they had fired a number of practice broadsides, the first naval gunfire heard in the bay since 1690, when Pierre Le Moyne D'Iberville's French ships sank the British ship *Hampshire* after a fierce battle.

Among the military officers aboard the destroyers were two officers who were VIPs in both a military and a diplomatic sense. Royal Navy Captain Sir Robert Stirling Hamilton was the naval attaché in the United Kingdom High Commissioner's office in Ottawa, and US Navy Captain Ben Scott Custer was his counterpart in the United States Embassy. Both had seen extensive service in the Second World War: Stirling Hamilton as a submarine commander in the Pacific, and Custer as commander of an aircraft carrier in the war against Japan.

Both were tall and lean. Stirling Hamilton was the traditional reserved British naval officer, but with a considerable streak of humour. Custer was more outgoing. He had a southern accent and a wide grin when he was questioned about his name. "No suh," he drawled. "Ahm no kin to the late unfortunate colonel of cavalry."

The US Navy had sent a twin Beechcraft, with Lieutenant Charles Wilcox and Chief Petty Officer Jack Kastner as crew, to transport the two captains to Ottawa. They planned to take off from Churchill and proceed to The Pas for refueling, before going east to Ottawa via Winnipeg. The reception over, the press were to return to Winnipeg in an RCAF Dakota.

On the morning of the flight, 12 September, the crew was joined by a fifth man, Master Sergeant Jerome Scalise, US Army Engineers, of Cambridge, Massachusetts, who was going home to retirement after thirty years in the service.

The RCAF press plane took off first and made a rough trip to Winnipeg through worsening weather. The Beechcraft, with five men and all their gear aboard, left a few minutes later. It never reached The Pas.

As soon as it became apparent that the Beechcraft's fuel endurance had expired, search orders were issued by the RCAF. No communication had been received from the missing plane, and aircraft from both Churchill and The Pas started to retrace the intended route.

Roy Brown, an experienced bush pilot who had been flying in the area, reported he had been forced to abandon his planned flight when the cloud ceiling lowered to less than 300 feet (91m).

By Tuesday, 14 September, men and aircraft from all over Canada were converging on The Pas where a search headquarters had been set up under the command of Group Captain Louis Z. Leigh, the RCAF's searchmaster. Named Operation Attaché, the search organization centred on Clearwater Lake Airport, northeast of The Pas.

Clearwater was built during the Second World War by the US Air Transport Command as a staging point on the proposed Winnipeg–The Pas–Churchill–Baffin Island–Greenland–Iceland–Britain route to evacuate casualties from the 1944 invasion of Hitler's Europe. Its frame and tarpaper buildings, vacant since 1945, were once again filled with air and ground crews as forty aircraft arrived to take part in what had quickly become Canada's biggest air search.

Lancasters, Flying Fortresses, Cansos, Dakotas, Norseman, and Grumman planes from the RCAF, US Navy, US Coast Guard, and US Army Air Corps were supplemented by a number of civilian planes in the region. Thousands of litres of aviation fuel arrived daily at The Pas by rail, along with cold-weather clothing, extra beds, blankets, and food for the growing search force that soon reached three hundred.

After ten days of searching, Leigh was still optimistic and spoke of continuing the search until the snow fell. Search planes had already crisscrossed an area larger than the Beechcraft was likely to have travelled. In an effort to provide more thorough coverage, the US Navy sent a 45.7-metre (150 ft.) silvery, helium-filled airship on 24 September. The blimp never got a chance to join the search, however. On that day the missing men were found 386 kilometres (240 mi.) northwest of The Pas on the very edge of what the searchers considered to be the limits of the downed plane's flying range. What had happened to put the Beechcraft so far off its planned route?

According to Captain Custer the weather they encountered after takeoff was terrible, with low cloud ceilings, turbulence, rain, snow, and ice. The magnetic compass began gyrating wildly and atmospheric disturbance made it impossible to receive more than one radio bearing, which indicated they were so far off track that they didn't believe it.

As their fuel ran out, Kastner, the most experienced pilot, set the plane down on what looked like a level green field, but what in reality was a stretch of knee-deep muskeg. The five men waded through the slimy muck to a stand of trees that promised higher, drier ground, and set up camp.

A survey of their equipment revealed that, among other things, they had a twenty-two-calibre rifle with forty-eight rounds of ammunition, three thirty-eight-calibre pistols with fifty rounds, a fishing rod and tackle, and two signal pistols with cartridges. They also had a thermos of coffee and one of water, sixteen sandwiches, and some chocolate, jam, and stale cake.

Scalise proved to be a most valuable member of the group. His steel helmet was useful for boiling water and cooking food, his hunting knife was invaluable, and his canvas sheet came in handy, as did his canteen and water bottle. He was also a veritable treasure trove of vital information about bush lore and living, his ingenuity producing many amenities that made life a little more bearable during the ten days the men were lost.

Custer thought they had been carried by the wind south and east and that they were east of Lake Winnipeg. Stirling Hamilton, however, using the hand compass and his watch, announced they were at about 105 degrees west longitude. He was right, within 32 kilometres (20 mi.).

After several days at their first camp, they decided they would have to rescue themselves, since they had seen no sign of search planes. The country through which they trekked, heading southwest, was rough and wild, and in many places, fire-damaged trees had fallen in a frustrating tangle of criss-crossed trunks and limbs. Some days they travelled less than 13 kilometres (8 mi.). They survived by eating a porcupine, grouse, squirrels, blueberries, and mushrooms. As they went south they laid out sections of parachute cloth in the shape of arrows to indicate the direction in which they were travelling, a clever tactic that turned out to be their salvation.

By 24 September, the twelfth day after their forced landing, they were still struggling through jackstrawed timber when they saw an aircraft some distance away. Later, a Canso amphibian of the RCAF flew over them. The first plane they had seen, an RCAF Lancaster, had found their downed Beechcraft. The Canso came to the scene and followed their marker panels to where they were. The Canso flew them to The Pas on the morning of Saturday, 25 September. On stepping out of the aircraft Custer said, "Thanks to God and the Royal Canadian Air Force five men are alive today who would not otherwise be alive."

Custer, Stirling Hamilton, Scalise, and Wilcox were flown back to Ottawa to be reunited with family and friends. Kastner volunteered to fly back to the scene of their landing to salvage all of their personal belongings, which had been left in the Beechcraft. He then burned the plane where it lay in the muskeg.

Both the senior officers had high praise for the abilities and energy of the three other members of the party, and Custer said he would recommend them for official commendations by the services they represented.

The exercise was an expensive one. Search planes covered close to 1.3 million square kilometres (500,000 sq. mi.). The search planes used more than 408,000 litres (90,000 gal.) of aviation fuel, and large quantities of food and other supplies were consumed. It was generally estimated the search had cost close to a million dollars.

How the Beechcraft came to be so far from where it was supposed to be, why their compasses behaved so erratically, and why Kastner was sent back to destroy the downed plane are questions no one has answered satisfactorily, and this has led to imaginative speculation.

The search itself, however, was well organized and, fortunately, successful, with a distinctly international and multi-service character.

TLC on the HBR

A winter view from the train car from which nursing services were provided on the Hudson Bay Railroad.

PHYLLIS MARTIN

Phyllis Martin was a member of the nursing staff in the hospital at Snow Lake in the 1950s when she read a newspaper advertisement that changed her life. The ad read: "NURSE WANTED. To take charge of Red Cross Nursing Services Car on the Hudson Bay Railway in Northern Manitoba. As this is the only position of its kind in Canada, it offers a unique opportunity for nurses. For full particulars apply immediately to: Director of Nursing Services, Manitoba Division, The Canadian Red Cross Society, 226 Osborne Street North, Winnipeg, Manitoba."

Years later Phyllis Martin wrote and published, at her own expense, an illustrated, thirty-six page booklet on her experiences as the Bay Line nurse. In it she wrote: "My application was in the next mail. At the time, I had been working as a registered nurse for eight years and before training, had lived and worked in the Indian Residential School at Norway House for three years. Through my previous experience, I felt well suited for this." Martin was also a gold-medal graduate of the St. Boniface General Hospital School of Nursing.

She received an immediate reply from the Red Cross, and by early August 1955, she was in Winnipeg for a two-week orientation course. The course included five days with a public health nurse in a small settlement east of Winnipeg, meetings with various officials of public health services, and the issue of a uniform. "I was fitted with a grey worsted suit and matching beret, a trenchcoat and a parka, both of which would later provide me with some soggy, cold moments. I was also issued with a supply of blue smocks to be worn in the clinic. Finally, I was given a handshake and a train ticket to Wabowden. My life on the Bay Line was about to begin."

The Bay Line—the Hudson Bay Railway to give it its official title—had been built in fits and starts from 1913 to 1929. The Canadian Northern (later to become part of the Canadian National Railway) reached The Pas in 1910. By 1913, as the result of an election promise, work was started on the long-awaited line to Hudson Bay.

Originally the tidewater terminus was to have been Port Nelson, at the mouth of the Nelson River and near the old HBC main trade centre at York Factory. But studies of possible locations and the viability of their harbours finally brought about a decision to divert the railway to Churchill, 160 kilometres (99 mi.) farther north.

According to Martin, she was the third nurse to be in charge of the Red Cross Car, which had been put into service in 1953 as the result of co-operation between the Canadian Red Cross, the Canadian National Railway, and the Manitoba government. The car had been sitting idle since her predecessor had left, and its condition called for considerable cleaning before it was ready for business.

Martin's first patient was a boy who had fractured his leg jumping over a fence. She was able to give him aid and then send him to The Pas for full medical treatment. Her next assignment was a visit to a school where she found deplorable conditions, including an infestation of head lice and totally unacceptable toilets for the children's use. Some quite energetic and stringent methods were called for, she felt, and she succeeded in getting the situation cleaned up. "My next visit to that particular school gave me satisfaction," she wrote later, "thanks to the efforts of the teachers. It took a few visits from the nurse and steady lecturing by the teachers, but conditions did improve."

The Red Cross Car was scheduled to be to be stationed in three-month stints alternatively at Wabowden and Gillam. For visits to other communities, Martin made use of whatever mode of transport was available. She undertook frequent trips on the scheduled trains that operated between The Pas and Churchill and side trips by boat, truck, Bombardier, and on one occasion, by helicopter. Once, she even rode the footplates of a steam engine pulling a passenger train because the day coach was full.

Two major tasks that Martin undertook during her time on the line were conducting immunization programs and administering the Salk polio vaccine. She also made frequent use of penicillin, which was then referred to as the "miracle drug."

The Salk vaccine program, conducted because of the polio outbreak of 1956, called for a considerable supply of sterile hypodermic needles. The drug also had to be kept at a temperature from zero to four degrees Celsius. Keeping the drug in a suitable condition created something of a problem for Martin since she often had to travel considerable distances from the car to the settlements where the children were to be treated.

"Finally," she wrote, "someone came up with a solution. The Red

Cross picked up the vaccine from the Health Department and put it into a Thermos flask. Then all we needed was a responsible person to deliver it to me." There was, it seemed, no lack of such persons. The first delivery was made by a dentist who was travelling on the Bay Line to hold clinics at various small centres; later, a CN porter volunteered his services.

Dr. Maxwell Bowman, director of preventative medical services for the provincial health department, sent Martin a directive authorizing her to administer the vaccine. The letter included complete instructions, one of which said the area where the injection was to be given should be wiped with iodine. Martin wrote: "I never liked iodine because it stains so badly," so she questioned the doctor about why it was specified. He replied that it was his experience that most of the children she would be treating regarded the shots as a welcome break in their normal routine and enjoyed the attention, so they would go to the back of the line, ready to receive a second dose. "I was glad for his advice," Martin wrote, "because I caught a few [children] trying that very stunt."

After the needles were used, they were washed and sharpened if needed, then wrapped up and sent back to the Red Cross in Winnipeg to be sterilized.

Martin's first experience with a helicopter came when two men arrived at the Red Cross Car from a bush camp some distance away. They reported that many of the men in the crew were feeling ill and asked if she would come to see them. Since a helicopter offered the only way of making the trip in the shortest time possible, she agreed to accompany them. She found several men in the camp feeling generally sick and discovered that they were suspicious of the water available and had not been drinking enough fluids.

She took a sample of the water and sent it to be tested in Winnipeg where it was approved for human use. The problem, she said, was that these men were doing heavy work in hot weather, plagued by mosquitoes and blackflies, and were simply dehydrated.

Life as a nurse in charge of the Red Cross Car was never dull. Among the varied emergencies and experiences that Martin had to cope with were:

- a large, heavy fish hook deeply embedded in a man's head, which took the combined efforts of the nurse and a visiting dentist to remove;

- a midnight-emergency call to an isolated cabin where a very sick baby was reported to be. When she arrived, Martin found the baby had died of pneumonia and had to call the RCMP to handle the legal details;

- a visit to the car in July 1956 by Manitoba Premier Douglas L. Campbell and several cabinet ministers and MLAs. Martin had been somewhat apprehensive beforehand, but, she said, "All seemed very interested and the whole affair was very pleasant"; and

- dealing with a supply of so-called "health biscuits "sent by the federal Department of Indian Affairs to improve nutrition of the schoolchildren. The biscuits were hard and dry and, after the first day's testing by the youngsters, found to be infested with worms. Martin dumped the biscuits into the bush. "Strangely," she wrote, "the town dogs were slow in finding them but when they did, dogs came from far and wide to enjoy the feast."

By August 1958, Martin was convinced that the service she was giving along the Bay Line could be provided from The Pas more efficiently and at less cost. The Red Cross agreed with her views and she obtained a suite in The Pas. She then proceeded to carry out her duties using regular train service supplemented by trips in boats and railway gas cars, neither of which were very enjoyable since they always seemed to be necessary in bad weather.

Her term in the north finished at the end of 1958. At that time she was informed that the provincial government was setting up a Northern Health Services program with a resident doctor, four public health nurses, and the necessary clerical staff. She was offered a job with this group but decided she wanted to widen her experience and instead obtained a job in a Winnipeg hospital.

During her four years on the Bay Line, Martin travelled thousands of miles, gave more than five thousand immunization and Salk vaccine shots, taught a number of first-aid and baby-care classes in the schools, and met thousands of people of all sorts.

Martin was forced to retire in 1975 because of illness, but she was able to put down some of her experiences and comments in her booklet entitled, *Red Cross Nurse on the Bay Line*.

Manitoba History Timeline

1610	**3 August**	Henry Hudson sails the *Discovery* into Hudson Bay.
1611	**21 June**	Mutiny on the *Discovery*. Hudson is set adrift and never seen again.
1612	**15 August**	Thomas Button finds and names the Nelson River.
1619	**5 September**	Jens Munk sails into Churchill Harbour in the *Unicorn*.
1668	**September**	The *Nonsuch* arrives at Rupert River on Hudson Bay.
1670	**2 May**	King Charles II creates Rupert's Land.
1738	**24 September**	De la Vérendrye builds Fort Rouge at the forks of the Red and Assiniboine Rivers.
1779	**Winter**	The North West Fur Company is established in Montreal.
1809		The North West Company builds Fort Gibraltar at the forks of the Red and Assiniboine Rivers.
1793		Cuthbert Grant Senior establishes a North West Company post on the Assiniboine River above the mouth of the Souris River.
1811		Lord Selkirk purchases Assiniboia from the Hudson's Bay Company
1814	**8 January**	Miles Macdonell issues the "Pemmican Proclamation," which prohibits the export of food from the Selkirk Settlement.
1815	**15 June**	Nor'Wester Duncan Cameron convinces 140 colonists to abandon Selkirk.
1816	**19 June**	The Battle of Seven Oaks
1817	**Spring**	Lord Selkirk's armed forces reclaim Fort Douglas.
1821	**1 June**	The Hudson's Bay Company and the North West Company amalgamate.
1822	**18 April**	Fort Gibraltar is renamed Fort Garry to honour Nicholas Garry.
1823	**10 June**	St. John's, the first Anglican church in Manitoba, is consecrated.
1824		Cuthbert Grant establishes Grantown, now known

as St. Francois Xavier.

1826 28 April   The greatest recorded flood in the history of Manitoba occurs.

1826   George Simpson is appointed the acting Governor-in-Chief of Rupert's Land.

1834   The Hudson's Bay Company re-purchases Assiniboia from the Selkirk estate.

1844 22 October   Louis Riel is born at St. Boniface.

1847 17 May   The results of the Pierre Sayer trial, which gave assent to free trade in furs, challenge the Hudson's Bay Company's trade monopoly.

1850   The Battle of the Grand Coteau between the Sioux and Red River buffalo hunters takes place on the Souris plains.

1859 10 June   *The Anson Northup* becomes the first steamboat on the Red River.

1859 28 December   The first edition of the *Nor'Wester* is published at Red River.

1867 1 July   Confederation

1869 November   Louis Riel and his men take Fort Garry; a provisional government is formed

1869 27 December   Louis Riel is elected president of the provisional government.

1870 4 March   Louis Riel orders Thomas Scott executed.

1870 15 July   Province of Manitoba enters Confederation; Winnipeg becomes the capital of both Manitoba and the Northwest Territories.

1870 August   The Red River Expedition claims Fort Garry. Louis Riel flees to the United States.

1870 30 December   The first election is held for the province's Legislative Assembly.

1871 15 March   The first session of the first Legislature is held.

1872 9 November   *The Manitoba Free Press* issues its first edition.

1873 8 November   The City of Winnipeg is incorporated

1876 7 October   The Northwest Territories Act is passed, separating it from Manitoba.

1877 28 February   The University of Manitoba receives its charter.

1883 11 December   Manitoba adopts Standard time.

1885	**17 March**	Louis Riel is elected president of the Provisional Government in the Northwest Territories. The Northwest Rebellion begins.
1885	**9–12 May**	The Battle of Batoche
1885	**15 May**	Louis Riel is taken prisoner.
1885	**June**	Chief Big Bear is taken prisoner.
1885	**16 November**	Louis Riel is executed in Regina.
1912	**26 February**	Manitoba's current boundaries are established.
1916	**27 January**	The Women's Suffrage Bill takes effect, making Manitoba women the first in Canada to vote and hold provincial office.
1916	**13 March**	Manitoba introduces prohibition under the Manitoba Temperance Act.
1918	**11 October**	Spanish Influenza reaches epidemic proportions. A ban is placed on public meetings in Manitoba.
1919	**April 5**	The Greater Winnipeg Aqueduct is completed.
1919	**15 May–21 June**	The Winnipeg General Strike
1919	**21 November**	The Golden Boy is placed on the dome of the Legislative Building.
1923	**June**	Prohibition ends and the Liquor Control Commission is enacted.
1929	**3 April**	The Last Spike is driven on the Hudson Bay Railway at Churchill.
1929	**4 October**	The Great Depression begins
1939	**10 September**	Canada declares war on Germany.
1945	**7 May**	Manitobans celebrate VE Day.
1950	**April–May**	Major flooding occurs in southern Manitoba.
1952		Women are permitted to sit on juries in Manitoba courts.
		Manitoba aboriginals are given the right to vote provincially.
1956		Stephen Juba becomes the first non–Anglo-Saxon mayor in Winnipeg.
1966		The Greater Winnipeg Floodway (Duff's Ditch) is officially opened.
1967		Winnipeg hosts the Pan Am Games.
		The University of Winnipeg and Brandon University are founded.

1972 1 January	Unicity is formed, making Winnipeg the first large Canadian city to rely on a single municipal administration for its whole metropolitan area.
1979 22 January	Former Manitoba premier Edward Schreyer becomes Canada's twenty-second Governor-General.
1980 27 August	*The Winnipeg Tribune* folds after ninety years of publication.
1983 Fall	Manitobans reject provincial establishment of French language rights and services by plebiscite.
1985 June	The Supreme Court of Canada renders Manitoba's "English-only" laws invalid.
1988 18 December	Gary Filmon announces that Manitoba does not support the Meech Lake Accord, saying that English language rights are restricted in Quebec.
1990 22 June	NDP MLA Elijah Harper kills the Meech Lake deal in his seventh refusal to allow debate on the accord to proceed in the Manitoba legislature.
1992 26 October	61.7 per cent of Manitobans vote against the Charlottetown Accord, one of the highest "no" votes in Canada.
1993 23 January	Métis leader Yvon Dumont becomes Lieutenant-Governor of Manitoba, 108 years after Louis Riel was hanged.
1997 May	About 25,000 people are forced from their homes when the Red River floods.
1999	Gary Filmon steps down after eleven years as premier, serving during the tumultuous Meech Lake and Charlottetown Accords.
2003 10 October	Winnipeggers honour the life of Winnipeg philanthropist and media mogul, Israel Asper.

Based on charts in *Manitoba 125: A History.* Winnipeg, MB: Great Plains Publications, 1993.

Index

About Fifth House

Fifth House Publishers, a Fitzhenry & Whiteside company, is a proudly western-Canadian press. Our publishing specialty is non-fiction as we believe that every community must possess a positive understanding of its worth and place if it is to remain vital and progressive. Fifth House is committed to "bringing the West to the rest" by publishing approximately twenty books a year about the land and people who make this region unique. Our books are selected for their quality, saleability, and contribution to the understanding of western-Canadian (and Canadian) history, culture, and environment.

Look for the following Fifth House titles at your local bookstore: